Eccentric Preachers

(Spurgeon's Shilling Series)

Charles H. Spurgeon

Bibliographical Information

Eccentric Preachers was originally published by Passmore & Alabaster, London, England, 1879.

an Ichthus Publications edition

ISBN 10: 1500773379
ISBN 13: 978-1500773373

www.ichthuspublications.com

Contents

Preface   *5*

1 What Is Eccentricity?   *7*

2 Who Have Been Called Eccentric?   *20*

3 Causes of Eccentricity   *34*

4 Hugh Latimer, 1480—1555   *49*

5 Hugh Peters, 1599—1660   *52*

6 Daniel Burgess, 1645—1713   *55*

7 John Berridge, 1716—1793   *58*

8 Rowland Hill, 1744—1833   *61*

9 Matthew Wilks, 1746—1829   *65*

10 William Dawson, 1773—1841   *69*

11 Jacob Gruber, 1778—1850   *73*

12 Edward Taylor, 1793—1871   *84*

13 Edward Brooke, 1779—1871   *89*

14 Billy Bray, The Uneducated Soul-winner   *96*

Conclusion   *103*

Eccentric Preachers

Preface

I HAVE PUBLISHED THIS little volume very much in self-defense. Some years ago I delivered a lecture on "Eccentric Preachers," and a reporter's notes of it were published in one of the newspapers. These, like all such things, were mere pickings and cuttings, and by no means the lecture itself. Gentlemen of the press have an eye to the amusement of their readers, and make selections of all the remarkable anecdotes, or odd sayings, used by a speaker, and when these are separated from their surroundings the result is anything but satisfactory. No man's speeches or lectures should be judged of by an ordinary newspaper summary, which in any case is a mere sketch, and in many instances is a vile caricature.

I thought no more of my lecture till the other day I found the mere rags and bones of the reporter set forth in America as an address by myself, worthy to be bound up with my book upon "Commenting and Commentaries." Those notes were all very well for a newspaper, but I altogether disown them as my production. It amazes me that the American editor should not have corrected the more obvious mistakes of the reporter, such as calling Peter Cartwright Peter *Garrett,* and Lady Ann Askew Lady *Askayne.* Peter Cartwright was an American backwoods preacher, and his name should have been familiar to the American editor, but some publishers are so intent upon getting out their books that they cannot afford time for correction.

Finding that I had by me the whole of the mutilated lecture, I thought of printing it, to show what I had really spoken; but upon looking it over, I judged it to be better to expand it and make it into a small book. I hope the reader will not be a loser by my resolution.

I desire by this little volume to plead against the carping spirit which makes a man an offender for a word, and the lying spirit which scatters falsehood right and left, to the injury and grief of the most zealous of my Master's servants. Many hearers lose much blessing through criticizing too much, and meditating too little; and many more incur great sin by calumniating those who live for the good of others. True pastors have enough of care and travail without being burdened by undeserved and useless fault-finding. We have something better to do than to be for ever answering every malignant or frivolous slander which is set afloat to injure us. We expected to prove our ministry "by evil report and by good report," and we are not therefore overwhelmed by abuse as though some new thing had happened unto us; and yet there are tender, loving spirits who feel the trial very keenly, and are sadly hindered in brave service by cruel assaults. The rougher and stronger among us laugh at those who ridicule us, but upon others the effect is very sorrowful. For their sakes are these pages written; may they be a warning to wanton witlings who defame the servants of the Most High God.

As ministers we are very far from being perfect, but many of us are doing our best, and we are grieved that the minds of our people should be more directed to our personal imperfections than to our divine message. God has purposely put his treasure in earthen vessels that the excellency of the power should be ascribed to himself alone: we beseech our hearers not to be so occupied with the faults of the casket as to forget the jewel. Wisdom is justified of her children, and grace works by such instruments as it pleases. Reader, be it yours to profit by all my Master's servants, and even by

Yours truly,
C. H. SPURGEON.

1
What Is Eccentricity?

OUGHT I NOT TO BE very timid in speaking upon eccentric preachers when I am somewhat sarcastically requested by an anonymous letter writer to *look at home?* I do look at home, and I am glad that I have such a happy home to look at. Trembling has not seized upon me upon receiving my nameless friend's advice, for two reasons; first, because I am not horrified by being charged with eccentricity, and secondly, because I do not consider myself to be guilty of that virtue or vice, whichever it may be. Years ago I might have been convicted of a mild degree of the quality, but since so many have copied my style, and so considerable a number have borrowed my discourses, I submit that I am rather the orthodox example than the glaring exception. After having lived for a quarter of a century in this region, I am not now regarded in London as a phenomenon to be stared at, but as an old-fashioned kind of body, who is tolerated as an established part of the ecclesiastical life of this vast city. Having moved in one orbit year after year without coming into serious collision with my neighbors I have reason to believe that my pathway in the religious heavens is not eccentric, but is as regular as that of the other lights which twinkle in the same sky. I have probably done my anonymous correspondent more honor than he deserves in taking so much notice of him; indeed, I only mention the man and his communication that I might bear witness against all anonymous letters. Never write a letter to which you are ashamed to put your name; as a rule, only mean persons are guilty of such an action, though I hope my present correspondent is an exception to the rule. Be so eccentric as to be always able to speak the truth to a man face to face. And now to our subject.

It is not the most profitable business in the world to find fault with our fellows. It is a trade which is generally followed by those who would excuse themselves from self-examination by turning their censures upon others. The beam in their own eye does not appear to be quite so large while they can discover motes in other men's optics, and hence they resort to the amusement of detraction. Ministers are the favorite prey of critics, and on Sundays, when they think it right to talk religion, they keep the rule to the letter, but violate its sense by most irreligiously overhauling the persons, characters, sayings and doings of God's servants. "Dinner is over. Bring the walnuts, and let us crack the reputations of a preacher or two. It is a pious exercise for the Sabbath." Then tongues move with abounding clatter; tales are told without number, and when the truth has been exhausted a few "inventions" are exhibited. One saw a preacher do what was never done, and another heard him say what was never said. Old fictions are brought up and declared to have happened a few days ago, though they never happened at all, and so the good people hallow the Sabbath with pious gossip and sanctimonious slander. There is a very serious side to this when we remember the fate of those who love and make a lie; but just now we will not dwell upon that solemn topic, lest we should be accused of *lecturing* our audience in more senses than one. So far as I am personally concerned, if the habit we are speaking of were not a sin, I do not know that I should care about it, for after having had more than my fair share of criticism and abuse, I am not one jot the worse for it in any respect; no bones are broken, my position is not injured, and my mind is not soured.

From the earliest period it has been found impossible for the messengers whom God has sent to suit their style of utterance to the tastes of all. In all generations useful preachers of the gospel have been objected to by a portion of the community. Mere chips in the porridge may escape censure and mildly win the tolerance of indifference, but decided worth will be surrounded with warm friends and red-hot foes. He who hopes to preach so as to please everybody must be newly come into the ministry; and he who aims at such an object would do well speedily to leave its ranks. Men must and will cavil and object: it is their nature to do so. John came neither eating nor drinking; he was at once a Baptist and an abstainer, and nothing could be alleged against his habits, which were far removed from the indulgences of luxury: but this excellence was made his fault, and they said, "He hath a devil." Jesus Christ came eating and drinking, living as a man among men; and this which they pretended to desire in John became an offense in Jesus, and they libeled him as "a drunken man and a winebibber, a friend of publicans and sinners." Neither the herald nor his Master suited the wayward tastes of their contemporaries. Like children playing in the market-place, who would not agree about what the game should be, so were the sons of men in that generation. They rejected the messengers because they loved not the God who sent them, and they only pretended to object to the men because they dared not avow their enmity to their Master. Hence the objections were often inconsistent and contradictory, and always frivolous and vexatious.

Filled with the same spirit of contrariety, the men of this world still depreciate the ministers whom God sends them and profess that they would gladly listen if different preachers could be found. Nothing can please them, their cavils are dealt out with heedless universality. Cephas is too blunt, Apollos is too flowery, Paul is too argumentative, Timothy is too young, James is too severe, John is too gentle. Nevertheless, wisdom is justified of all her children. At this time, when God raises up a man of original mind who strikes out a course for himself and follows it with success, it is usual to charge him with being eccentric. If his honesty may not be suspected, nor his zeal questioned, nor his power denied, sneer at him and call him *eccentric,* and it may be the arrow will wound.

Let us now pay our attention to this dreadful word *eccentric,* and then see by what means it has been fixed upon certain preachers of the gospel, and those not the least in usefulness.

What is it to be eccentric? The short and easy method for determining the meaning of a word is to go to the dictionary. Dr. Samuel Johnson, what say you? The sage replies, "It signifies deviating from the center, or not having the same center as another circle." The gruff lexicographer proves his definition by quoting from an astronomer who charges the sun with eccentricity. "By reason of the sun's eccentricity to the earth and obliquity to the equator, it appears to us to move unequally." Eccentric preachers are evidently in brilliant society. Now I am free to admit that the word has come to mean singular, odd, whimsical, and so forth; but by going a little deeper into its etymology, we discover that it simply means that the circle in which an eccentric man moves is not quite coincident with that which is followed by the majority: he does not tread the regular ring, but deviates more or less as he sees fit. It would be easy to prove that a movement may be eccentric, and yet quite regular and effective. Every man who has to do with machinery knows what it is for one wheel to be eccentric to another, and he knows also that often this may be a needful and useful arrangement for the purpose of the machine. It does not seem so very horrible after all that a man should be eccentric. I suppose the popular meaning is that a man is off the circle, or in more vulgar phrase, "off the square." But the point is, who is to tell us what the square is, and who is to decide which circle a man is bound to follow? True, this second circle is not concentric with the first, but it is not therefore more eccentric than the first, for each one is eccentric to the other. It may be that A. is eccentric to B., but B. is quite as much eccentric to A. A man called me a Dissenter the other day, and I admitted that I dissented from him, but I charged him with being a Dissenter because he dissented from me. He replied that I was a Nonconformist, but I retorted that he also was a Nonconformist, for he did not conform to me. Such terms, if they are to be accurately employed, require a fixed standard; and in the case of the term "eccentricity" we need first to settle a center and a circumference, from which we may depart. This will be no easy task: indeed, those who attempt it will find it to be impossible in matters of taste and deportment, according to the old adage, *"de gustibus,* etc.," (concerning matters of taste it is idle to dispute), and the well-worn proverb, "every man to his taste."

In morals conscience has fixed the center and struck the ring; and in religion revelation has used the compasses and given us a perfect sphere. God grant that we may not be eccentric towards God, either as to holiness or truth, for that were fatal: but when fashion and custom mark out ill-proportioned imitations of the circle of perfection, or even dare to impose curves of their own, it may be grandly right to be eccentric, for an eccentric path all the saints have trodden as they have tracked the narrow way in the teeth of the many who pursue the downward road.

From such consecrated eccentricity come martyrs, reformers, and the leaders of the advance guard of freedom and progress. Breaking loose from the shackles of evil customs, such men first stand alone and defy the world; but ere long the great heart of manhood discerns their excellence, and then men are so eager to fall at their feet that the idolatry of hero-worship is scarcely escaped. To us the men seem grander in their solitary adherence to the right, and to the true, than when they become the centers of admiration: their brave eccentricity is the brightest gem in their crown. The slavery of custom is as hard and crushing as any other form of human bondage, and blessed is he who for the truth's sake disdains to wear the galling chain, preferring rather to be charged with singularity and held up to ridicule. It is clear, then, that eccentricity may in certain cases be a virtue. When it touches the moral and the spiritual it may be worthy of all honor.

As to preachers and their mode of procedure, what is eccentricity? Who is to fix the center? I say to all those professed critics who tell us that certain preachers are eccentric—"Who is to fix the center for them?" Shall this important task devolve upon those gentlemen who buy lithographed sermons and preach them as their own? These men are in no danger of violating propriety in the excess of their zeal, for their discourses are cut and dried for them at wholesale establishments. Do you ask, "Is this true?" I answer, undoubtedly; for the other day, to test the matter, I sent my secretary to a certain bookseller's, and he brought home to me specimens of these precious productions, lithographed or written by hand, at prices descending from a shilling to sixpence each: a choke variety, believe me. Some of these invaluable discourses are carefully marked in places to indicate the degree of emphasis to be used, and spaces or dotted lines are employed to indicate the pauses and their suggested length. No one calls the users of these pretty things eccentric; are we, therefore, to regard them as the model preachers to whom we are to be conformed? Are we all to purchase spiritual food for our flocks, at the liberal rate of half a guinea a quarter for thirteen sermons, to be exchanged at Lady-day, Midsummer, Michaelmas, and Christmas? If these things be so, and this trade is to be continued and increased, I suppose that we who think out our own sermons, and deliver them fresh from our hearts, will be regarded as odd fellows, just as Mr. Wesley was stigmatized as eccentric because he wore his own hair when all the fashionable world rejoiced in wigs. Well, my brethren, if it should ever be the fashion to wear wooden legs I shall be eccentric enough to keep to those which nature gave me, weak as they are, and I trust that the number of eccentric people will be sufficient to keep me in countenance.

Who is to fix the center of the circle? Shall we give the compasses into the hand of the high-flying brethren whose rhetoric towers into the clouds and is shrouded and lost in them? Certainly these do the business very grandly, dealing in the sublime and beautiful quite as freely as Burke himself. No common man understandeth or so much as dareth to attempt understanding these gentlemen of the altitudes and profundities. Their big words are by no means needful on account of the greatness of their matter, but seem to be chosen upon the principle that the less they have to say the more pompous must be their phrases. In their magniloquence they:

> "Set wheels on wheels in motion—such a clatter—
> To force up one poor nipperkin of water!
> Broad ocean labors with tremendous roar,
> To heave a cockle-shell upon the shore.

Mr. Muchado is still engaged in whipping his creams into a froth of the consistency of half a nothing; and we may hear the Rev. Mr. Pretty-man in many a pulpit exercising the art of spread-eagle to a coterie who do not suspect him of eccentricity, but consider him to be the model divine.

Not in words only are the high-fliers comparable to masses of floating cloud, but in doctrine they are equally beyond all comprehension.

They are philosophical gentlemen, superior persons of special culture, though what has been cultivated in them, except an affectation of learning, it would be hard to say. They confuse those whom they ought to confirm, and stagger those whom they should establish. Bishop Blomfield tells us that a certain verger said to him, "Do you know I have been verger of this church fifty years, and though I have heard all the great sermons preached in this place I am still a Christian." Now, are these dealers in words and dreams to fix the center? If so, we intend to be eccentric; and blessed be God we are not alone in that resolve, for there are others who join with us in the opinion that to be studying the prettinesses of elocution, and the fancies of philosophy, while men are perishing around us is the brutal eccentricity of a Nero, who fiddled while Rome was burning and sent his galleys to fetch sand from Alexandria while the populace died for want of bread. If the center is to be up in the clouds, let a few of us who care for something practical stop down below and be regarded as eccentric. It is an odd thing that some men prefer to speak upon topics of which they know nothing, and from which no benefit can possibly arise, while themes which might edify are disregarded. Timbs tells us of an eccentric "Walking Stewart," who had perambulated half the world but would never talk of his travels, preferring to descant upon "The Polarity and Moral Truth," whereon he spoke so wildly that no one could make head or tail of it. Like this departed worthy, certain men are most at home when they are all abroad, and most important when their subject is insignificant. We do not choose their center, for it is far more suitable for will-o'-the-wisps than ministers of the eternal word. When all souls are saved and all mourners comforted we may venture to discuss recondite theories, but not while graveyards are filling with those who know not God.

    Where, then, is the center to be found? Am I directed to yonder vestry? I beg pardon—sacristy. If you will open that door, you will perceive a considerable number of cupboards, presses, and recesses. Where are we? Is this a milliner's shop, or a laundry, or both? Those linen garments reflect great credit upon the washerwoman and ironer; but the establishment is not a laundry, for here hang black gowns, and white gowns, and raiment as fine as Joseph's coat. And what a variety! Here, young man, fetch the ecclesiastical dictionary! Here we have an alb and an amice, a cope for the parson, and a corporal for the bread and wine, and—well, there's no end of the concerns! We are not well instructed in the terminology of these drapery establishments, but we are informed that these things are not to be treated with levity, seeing that therein abideth much grace, which ministereth to the establishment of the saints. In truth, we have small care to linger among these resplendent rags, but assuredly if the center of gravity lies with gentlemen who thus bedizen their corporeal frames, we prefer to be eccentric, and dress as other male humanities are wont to do. It has seemed to us to be needful to discard even the white necktie. While it was the ordinary dress of a gentleman, well and good; but as it has grown to denote a personage of the clerical sort, or in other words, has become a priestly badge, it seems best to abjure it. This may be done the more readily because it is also the favorite decoration of undertakers and waiters at hotels, and one has no wish to be taken for either of these deserving functionaries. Some young preachers delight in cravats of extreme length, and others tie them with great precision, reminding us of Beau Brummel, who produced miraculous ties, because, as he said, he gave his whole mind to them. I was much aided in the summary dismission of my tie by an incident which happened to me when I first came to London. I was crossing the river by a penny steamboat, when a rude fellow said to me, "How are you getting on at Hitchcock's?" I could not imagine what he meant; but he explained that he supposed I was in the drapery line, and was probably at that eminent firm. He tried hard to find out where I was serving, and when I gave him for answer that I knew none of the houses in the City, and was not in the drapery, "Then," said he, "you're a Methodist parson"; which was a better shot by far, and yet not quite a bull's-eye. Having no desire to be lifted into the clerical order, or to claim any distinction above my fellow church members, I dress as they dress, and wear no special distinguishing mark. Let men of sense judge whether this is one-half so eccentric as arraying one's self so that it is hard for spectators to guess whether you are a man or a woman, and very easy to say that your garnishing is not manly, but ostentatious, and oftentimes meretricious and absurd. The center is not here. They that wear soft raiment are in king's houses, but the King of kings cares nothing for the finery and foppery of ecclesiastical parade.

According to common talk, the center of the circle is fixed by the dullest of all the brotherhood, for to be eccentric means with many to have anything over half a grain of common sense, or the remotest favoring of humor. Have anything like originality, anything like genius, anything like a sparkle of wit, anything like natural whole-souled action, and you will be called eccentric directly by those who are used to the gospel of Hum-drum. The concentric thing with many is to prose away with great propriety and drone with supreme decorum. Your regular man says nothing which can by any possibility offend anybody, and nothing which is likely to do anyone good. Devoid of faults, and destitute of excellencies, the *proper* preacher pursues his mechanical round, and shudders at the more erratic motions of real life. Far be it from us to depreciate the excellent brother, his way is doubtless the best for him, yet are there other modes which are quite as commendable though more likely to be censured, If you will be as dry as sawdust, as devoid of juice as the sole of an old shoe, and as correct as the multiplication table, you shall earn to yourself a high degree in the great university of Droneingen, but if you wake up your soul and adopt an energetic delivery, and a natural, manly, lively, forcible mode of utterance, all the great authorities of that gigantic institution will say, "Oh dear, it is a pity he is so eccentric." Common sense decidedly objects to have the center for an eagle fixed by an owl, or the circle for a waxwork figure forced upon a living man.

As to this supposed center of the circle, which we have tried in vain to settle, it may be as well to remark that it is not fixed, and never can be fixed; for climes and times and circumstances involve perpetual change. Some hundred or more years ago Mr. John Wesley stood on his father's grave to preach in Epworth churchyard, and he was thought very eccentric for proclaiming the gospel in the open air; as for Mr. Whitefield, he was considered to be demented, or he would never have taken to the fields. Our Lord and his apostles had long before preached under the open heavens, and, persecuted as they were, no one in those days called them eccentric because of that particular practice; and, to show how the ideas of men have changed again, no one is now considered to be eccentric for open-air preaching, at least, not in these regions. I might preach standing on a gravestone to-morrow, and none would blame me. Yes, I forgot, it must not be in a national graveyard, or I should be liable to something dreadful. We must neither stand on an Episcopal tombstone nor be laid under one with our own funeral rites. Those orthodox worms which have fattened on correctly buried corpses so long, would be taken ill if they fed on bodies over which the regular chaplain has not asked a blessing. This care for the worms is to my mind rather eccentric, but let that pass, it will soon be numbered among the superstitions of a dark age. As times roll on, that which is eccentric in one era becomes general and even fashionable in another. The costume and general cut of a preacher of Queen Elizabeth's day would create a smile if it should be copied under the reign of Queen Victoria, and even the knee breeches, silk stockings, and silver buckles which I have myself seen upon my venerated grandfather would create many a smile if they were to reappear at the next meeting of the

Congregational Union. "The nasal twang learned at conventicle" was once regarded as the holy tone of piety, and yet the man who should use it now, if he were an Englishman, would be thought an odd being. Indeed, much of the oddity of the famous Matthew Wilks lay in that particular habit; he made you smile, even when speaking with all solemnity by the strangeness of his voice, and yet I never heard that our Puritanic ancestors were otherwise than grave while listening to the same peculiar form of utterance. Time was when it was accounted one of the outrageous deeds of a certain Jack Hanway, that he actually walked down a street in London on a rainy day, carrying a new-fangled kind of round tent to keep off the wet; yet no one quotes this action now as a proof of extreme eccentricity, for umbrellas are as common as mushrooms.

The following incident, which happened to myself, will show the power of race and climate in producing the charge of eccentricity. A Dutchman, who from the very orderly style of his handwriting, and the precision of his phrases, should be a very exemplary individual, once wrote me a sternly admonitory letter. From having read my printed discourses with much pleasure he had come to consider me as a godly minister, and, therefore, being in London, he had availed himself of the opportunity to hear me. This, however, he deeply regretted, as he had now lost the power to read my sermons with pleasure any more. What, think you, had I said or done to deprive me of the good opinion of so excellent a Hollander? I will relieve your mind by saying that he considered that I preached exceedingly well, and he did not charge me with any extravagances of action, but it was my personal appearance which shocked him. I wore a beard, which was bad enough, but worse than this, he observed upon my lip *a moustache!* Now this guilty thing is really so insignificant an affair that he might have overlooked such an unobtrusive offender. But, no, he said that I wore a moustache like a carnal, worldly-minded man! Think of that. Instead of being all shaven and shorn like the holy man whom he was accustomed to hear, and wearing a starched ruffed collar all round my neck, about a quarter of a yard deep, I was so depraved as to wear no ruff, and abjure the razor. His great guy of a minister, with ruff and bands and gown, and a woman's chin was *not* eccentric, but because I allowed my hair to grow as nature meant it should, I was eccentric and frivolous and carnal and worldly-minded, and all sorts of bad things. You see, what is eccentric in Holland is not eccentric in England, and *vice versa*. Much of the eccentric business is a matter of longitude and latitude, and to be quite correct one would need to take his bearings, and carry with him a book of costumes and customs, graduated according to the distance from the first meridian.

Moreover, we may not forget that as in religion there have been times of persecution, and times of toleration, so has it been with the pulpit. At one date propriety ruled supreme, and men were doomed to instant ostracism if they passed beyond the settled line; while at another date a sort of Eccentric Emancipation Act is passed, and every man does what is right in his own eyes. At the present moment great latitude is allowed, and several persons are now saying and doing very remarkable things, and yet are escaping the charge of eccentricity. It is well for them that some of us lived before them, and for far smaller liberties were set in the pillory. For myself, I venture to say that I have been severely criticized for anecdotes and illustrations of the very same kind which I meet with in the very excellent discourses of my friend, Mr. Moody, whom I appreciate probably more than anybody else. Many dear, good souls who have heard him with pleasure would not have done so twenty years ago, but would have regarded him as very eccentric. As to Mr. Sankey's singing, of which I equally approve, would not that have been unpardonable even ten years ago? Would Ned Wright and Joshua Poole, and brethren of that order, have been tolerated in 1858? According to the rules which judged Rowland Hill to be eccentric, I should say that these brethren are quite as far gone, if not further, and yet one does not hear an outcry against them for eccentricity. No, the bonds are relaxed, and it is just possible that they are now rather too slack than too tight. It is, however, very curious to watch the moods of the religious public and see how what is condemned to-day is admired tomorrow. Such an observation has a great tendency to make a man rise superior to the verdict of the period, and choose his own path. To promote a manly, courageous course of action in such matters is our main object in delivering this lecture.

Let us, if we are ministers, do that which we believe to be most likely to be useful, and pay little heed to the judgments of our contemporaries. If we act wisely we can afford to wait; our reward is in a higher approbation than that of men; but even if it were not, we can afford to wait. The sweeping censures of hurried critics will one day be blown away like the chaff of the threshing-floor, and the great heart of the church of God will beat true to her real champions, and clear their reputations from the tarnish of prejudice and slander. The eccentricity of one century is the heroism of another; and what is in one age cast out as folly may be in the next revered as a wisdom which lived before its time. Well said the apostle, "With me it is a very small thing that I should be judged of you, or of man's judgment: yea, I judge not mine own self."

To return to our circle and *con*centricity: It would be a very great pity if the center of the circle could be fixed by a decree like that of the Medes and Persians, which altereth not. If we could settle once for all what is concentric and what is eccentric, it would be a very serious evil, for the differences of utterance and modes of address among God's ministers serve a very useful purpose. When Dr. John Owen said that he would give all his learning to be able to preach like the tinker, John Bunyan, he spake not wisely, unless he meant no more than to extol honest John; for Owen's discourses, profound, solid, weighty, and probably heavy, suited a class of persons who could not have received Bunyan's delightfully illustrated preaching of the plain gospel. No, Dr. Owen, you had better remain Dr. Owen, for we could by no means afford to lose that mine of theological wealth which you have bequeathed to us. You would have looked very awkward if you had tried to talk like the marvelous dreamer, and he would have played the fool if he had imitated you. It is pitiful to hear comparisons made between the different servants of the same Lord. They were made by their Master, the one as well as the other, and set in different spheres to answer his own designs, and the same wisdom is displayed in each. I heard the other day of a discussion which may have answered its design in educating youthful powers of debate, but intrinsically it was an idle theme; it was this—does the world owe most to the printing press or to the steam engine? The machines are alike useful for the purposes intended, and both essential to the world's progress, why contrast them? Why not as well raise a controversy as to the relative values of needles and pins? Robert Robinson, of Cambridge, had a terse, vigorous, and somewhat homely style of preaching, and I heard it asserted that it was more effective than that of Robert Hall, by whom he was succeeded, who was grandly rhetorical and overwhelming. Who is to judge in such a matter? Who in his senses would even tolerate the question? We claim for Robert Hall a master's seat in the assembly of divines, nor would we place Robert Robinson below him, for each man suited the condition of the church. We admire every man in his own order, or even in his own disorder, so long as it is really his own. He has some end to serve in God's eternal purpose, let him answer that end without carping criticism from us. Who are we, that we should even condemn what seems to us odd and singular? How many souls were won to God by Mr. Rowland Hill's "eccentricities," as they called them, the judgment day alone will reveal. You have, doubtless, heard of the young

Eccentric Preachers

man who was about to go to India, and a pious friend was very anxious that he should not leave the country in an unconverted state. He induced this young man to stay a week with him in London, and took him to hear a minister of much repute, a very able man—a man of sound argument and solid thought, in the hope that perhaps something which he said would lead to his friend's conversion. The youth listened to the sermon, pronounced it an excellent discourse, and there was an end of it. He was taken to hear another earnest preacher, but no result came of the service. When the last night came, the godly friend, in a sort of desperation, ventured with much trembling to lead his companion to Surrey Chapel, to hear Mr. Hill, praying earnestly that Mr. Hill might not say any funny things; that he might, in fact, preach a very solemn sermon, and not say anything whatever that might cause a titter. To his horror, Mr. Hill that night seemed to be more than ever lively, and he said many quaint things. Among the rest he said that he had seen a number of pigs following a butcher in the street, at which he marvelled, inasmuch as swine have usually a will of their own, and that will is not often according to their driver's mind. Mr. Hill, upon inquiring, found that the aforesaid pigs followed the leader because he had peas in his pocket, and every now and then he dropped a few before them, thus overcoming their scruples and propensities. Even so, said Mr. Hill, does the devil lead ungodly men captives to his will, and conduct them into the slaughterhouse of everlasting destruction, by indulging them in the pleasures of the world. The sober gentleman who had brought his friend to the chapel was greatly shocked at such a groveling simile, and grieved to think of the mirth which his young friend would find in such a dreadful observation. They reached the door, and to his surprise the youth observed, "I shall never forget this service. That story about the pigs has deeply impressed me, for I fear it is my case." A happy conversion followed, and the critic could only retract his criticism in the silence of his own grateful heart. Well, then, let each servant of God tell his message in his own way. To his own Master he shall stand or fall.

If God moves a Rowland Hill to speak of pigs, it will be better than if he had descanted upon purling brooks, or blue-eyed seraphim. Taste may be shocked, but what of taste when men are to be aroused from the fatal slumbers of indifference! If you are living without Christ in the world, your state and condition are far more shocking in themselves than any arousing words can possibly be. It is sin which is vulgar and in bad taste; so they think who best can judge,—the purest of our race and the angels in heaven. It disgusts me to see a man whom God's word declares to be "condemned already" giving himself airs, and affecting to be too delicate to hear a homely sentence from one who desires to save him from eternal wrath. He is coarse enough to despise the altogether lovely One, brutal enough to reject the gospel of love, and base enough to rebel against his Creator and Preserver, and yet forsooth he is a connoisseur in religion, and picks over every word which is spoken to him for his good! This spiritual prudery is sickening to the last degree.

I have given the story of Mr. Hill because it is a type of many which are considered to be eccentric and coarse, but which are not so at all, except to shallow minds. There is nothing essentially vulgar in an allusion to pigs any more than to any other animals, for our Lord himself spoke of "casting pearls before swine," and the apostle Peter alluded to the sow that was washed wallowing in the mire. Nor is there anything essentially coarse in the simile of the hogs following the butcher; in fact, it is less coarse than Peter's metaphor which we have quoted, especially when coupled with the dog's returning to his vomit. No creature, truly represented, is common or unclean. It is only a sort of Phariseeism of taste which makes it so. Real vulgarity lies in foul allusions and indelicate hints, and these are to be found among men of dainty speech, such as Laurence Sterne, and not among holy and homely minds after the order of Rowland Hill. Tinge your stories or your figures with dirt, Mr. *Slop*dash! and we abandon you: nothing which is indelicate can be endured in the service of a holy God. Come home to the heart in your own genial, home-spun manner, and I, for one, will delight in you, Mr. *Slap*dash! and bid you God speed. So much difference is there between *slop* and *slap* that it might furnish a theme for a lecture, and yet there is only the change of a vowel in the words. So may disgusting vulgarity and homely force wear the same aspect, and yet they differ as much as black and white. There is a charming poetry in many a simple figure which unsophisticated minds delight in. If a smile is raised it only shows that the soul is awake, and is pleased to be taught so plainly. Critics may take out their penknives to gore and gash, but honest hearts delight in the natural expressions, the instructive comparisons, and the heartfelt utterances of the earnest man whom the world sets down as

AN ECCENTRIC PREACHER.

2
Who Have Been Called Eccentric?

IN THE PREVIOUS LECTURE we gained some little light upon the true meaning of eccentricity, and we discovered it in certain quarters where it is little suspected, while we saw many to be free from it who have been popularly charged with it. Let it not, however, be supposed that we shall attempt the justification of all eccentrics. We are sorrowfully compelled to concede to critics of the ministry that persons have entered it who have sadly disgraced our high calling. Men in all denominations have earned notoriety by being out of center morally and spiritually: these have deserved to be called eccentric in the worst sense. Now, while we stand up for the apostles, we expressly exclude Judas Iscariot. Find us a man who tries to attract attention by the affectation of oddity, who is a mere mountebank or mimic, and we have not a word to say in his defense, but we give him over as a dead horse to the dogs of criticism. They may rend him in pieces, and devour him if so they desire, for impostors and pretenders deserve the critic's sharpest teeth. Find us a preacher who obtains notoriety for himself by descending to buffoonery, and who goes out of his way to say smart things, and make jokes on sacred subjects, and we decline to be his advocate.

Natural humor may possibly be consecrated and made to wear the yoke of Christ, but he who apes it is no true man. If you find us a man who has any object in this world in what he says but the glory of God, and the winning of souls, he is the man who is out of center, and into his secret may we never come. And furthermore, if you discover a preacher who is indelicate, and causes the cheek of modesty to tingle, let him be cast out of the pulpit, and the door locked against him. We have known men of the Slop-dash order who would have been nothing if they had not been outrageous, and of these it may be said that they were worse than nothing when they followed their own style. There was nothing in their absurdities to excuse them, for they were not carried away by zeal, nor did the excellence of their matter make up for the ridiculousness of their manner. Of such men we will neither be defender nor judge.

We do not care whether he performs in the parish church or hangs out at a little Bethel, the man who shocks decency and plays the fool with solemn truths is unworthy of his office. I have heard that a certain preacher finding himself in Northamptonshire, among the shoemakers, in order to draw a congregation, gave notice in the morning that he would in the evening tell them the quickest way to make a pair of shoes. When they crowded the place, he bade them *take a pair of boots and cut the tops off.* If this was really done, then I say, let this wit among cobblers live and die at his trade, but let him not again go beyond his last. I had my doubts about this story, for I found it told both of Henley and of Hill, and I was morally certain that at least the second edition of it was an old tale new vamped; but I am sorry that I have met with an advertisement by Orator Henley which proves that he actually did this, not in Northampton, but in London, and headed his announcement with a Latin sentence signifying that the greater includes the less. We shall have more of this Orator Henley directly.

In my youth I remember the eccentric fame of a clergyman who lived near my father's house. He found himself at church one Sunday morning with a political pamphlet in his pocket instead of his sermon, and throwing it down into the churchwarden's pew, he bade him read a bit of it while he went home for his discourse. Many very questionable deeds were done by this parson of the old fox-hunting school, and his general manners fully entitled him to be called eccentric. It would be a pity to revive the stories told in many an Essex village thirty years ago of parsons and clerks of a race which ought to be speedily forgotten. Methodists and Ranters have been the song of the drunkard and the target of many fiery arrows, but never has anything been imputed to the indiscretion of their zeal which has been one-tenth as mischievous as were the evil lives of those who opposed them. I care not to say more; no section of the church can afford to throw stones, for no department has been free from unworthy ministers, adventurers, hypocrites, and downright fools.

Moderation is not the virtue of many. If one man casts a sprinkling of the salt of wit into his sermon straightway some half idiotic brother must set the people grinning all the sermon through. If one, to whom it is natural, is so carried away by his earnestness that his action becomes at times highly dramatic, instantly a certain crew fall to mouthing and posturing as if these things were the great power of God. If one man occasionally spiritualizes, but keeps within the bounds of discretion, they must needs indulge all sorts of fancies till one might say of them as a foreigner said of King James's favorite preacher, "He playeth with his text, patting it to and fro, as a cat doth a mouse." They put the wise man's wig upon their little skulls, and fancy that they have become as great as he. These hangers-on of useful men have not even the virtue of being the genuine article, they are counterfeits in which are exaggerated all the imperfections of the original, while all the excellencies are omitted.

One can hardly tell at this distance of time what to believe, and what to reject, of the character of Orator Henley, who flourished some hundred and thirty years ago in Butcher Row, Newport Market. If the representations of historians are correct he was an eccentric man of the class which disgusts all godly minds. He announced himself as "the restorer of ancient eloquence," and selected for his themes subjects religious, political, and personal. He was frequently prosecuted for libel, and never seemed to bridle his tongue on that account, but with low ribaldry and buffoonery he pursued the golden object which he had set before him. In an unfortunate moment he attacked the poet Pope, who in revenge held him up to scorn in his "Dunciad":—

> "Imbrown'd with native bronze, lo Henley stands,
> Tuning his voice, and balancing his hands,
> How fluent nonsense trickles from his tongue!
> How sweet the periods, neither said nor sung!
> Still break the benches, Henley, with thy strain,
> While Sherlock, Hare, and Gibson preach in vain.
> O great restorer of the good old stage,
> Preacher at once and zany of thy age!"

I say again that there is no knowing how far Henley deserved all this, but if report speaks truly he was a mournful instance of talent perverted to evil uses, and of self-conceit blown up to an amazing pitch. To such men the whip of scorpions, which Pope could handle so skillfully, was well applied.

Creatures of Henley's kind existed among the friar-preachers of the mediaeval period, whose ignorance and cunning were equally the ridicule of their contemporaries; though even among them there were true-hearted men whose singularities arose out of their zeal to do good. The genus of religious mountebank is not quite extinct at the present day, though seldom seen in such full development as in the friar period. Men of this order are generally known and read by the Christian public, and seldom gain either profit or honor from their wretched adventure; it were a pity that they should.

The miserable instances alluded to are often used as stones to throw at really gracious men, and the attempt to prove that all preachers are alike is repeated in the face of a thousand facts. Because some charlatans have been eccentric, therefore all eccentric men must be mere impostors; and this being taken for granted, the next thing to be done is to represent really sober-minded men as wild and singular, that so they also may be regarded as deceivers.

A reputation for eccentricity has been unjustly fastened upon many men by persistent falsehood. Throw enough mud and some of it will be sure to stick: upon this theory have good men been assailed. Whatever of originality and quaintness they have possessed has been grossly caricatured; and silly tales, the worthless legends of remote periods, have been revived and fathered upon them. It is interesting to trace the pedigree of a pulpit story, though it is not often possible to discover its actual parent: in fact, we believe that, like Topsy, many of these tales have no father nor mother, but may say of themselves, "'specs I growed." The rise and progress of a current falsehood, if well studied, would reveal a sad page in human history. The same anecdotes occur from age to age, but they are tacked on to different men. In the days when hour-glasses were affixed to many pulpits, to suggest a limit to long-winded discourses, it was natural that wags should invent humorous stories concerning them. One of them is set forth in a print which represents Hugh Peters preaching, and holding up an hourglass as he utters the words, "I know you are good fellows, so let us have another glass." It is probable that Peters never said this, and more than probable that if he did say something like it, the connection in which it was spoken set it in quite another light. However that may be, it was too good a story to be allowed to go out of use, and therefore it came to pass that in due time it was told with slight variation of Daniel Burgess, a celebrated Nonconformist divine, whose vigorous speech frequently made him enemies. Nor was this enough, for a very similar anecdote turned up a third time in a neighboring country, and this time it was a Presbyterian clergyman who used the expression, "Let us have another glass, and then"—when preaching before the High Commissioner. Happily for Rowland Hill and Matthew Wilks the hourglass was out of date in their day, or else they would have been represented as saying the same thing. Liars ought to have good memories that they may recollect that they have already assigned a story to someone else. A particle of creative genius might also render their work a little less monotonous.

I remember reading with some amusement of Lorenzo Dow, who is reported some sixty years ago to have slipped down a tree in the backwoods, in order to illustrate the easiness of backsliding. He had previously pulled himself up with extreme difficulty, in order to show how hard a thing it is to regain lost ground. I was all the more diverted because it has so happened that this pretty piece of nonsense has been imputed to myself. I was represented as sliding down the banisters of my pulpit, and that at a time when the pulpit was fixed in the wall and was entered from behind! I never gave even the remotest occasion for that falsehood, and yet it is daily repeated, and I have heard of persons who were present when I did so, and, with their own eyes, saw me perform the silly trick. It is possible for a person to repeat a falsehood so many times that he at length imposes upon himself and believes that he is stating the truth. Here is the original tale, extracted from Mr. Taylor's "Model Preacher":—

> "A man once went to Vincennes, in the United States, to hear Lorenzo Dow preach on backsliding. He said, 'An immense concourse of people assembled in the woods, and waited for Dow's arrival. Finally he made his appearance, and at the time all expected the sermon he arose, climbed up a smooth sapling, and cried out, 'Hold on there, Dow; hold on.' He soon slid down to the ground, and put on his hat and left. That was all the sermon we heard that day."

If this was all the sermon it certainly left a great deal for the hearer to work out, and it reminds us of the Welsh preacher who, with almost as little speaking, forcibly brought a great question before his people. He ascended the pulpit on the Sunday morning, looked around him and said, "My brethren, I shall ask you a question which neither you nor I can answer— 'What shall it profit a man if he gain the whole world and lose his own soul?'" When he had thus spoken he left the pulpit, walked down the aisle, and went home. If the hearers did not think that morning it was no fault of his. I wonder that some one has not told this story of me; perhaps they think it too good.

It was reported of Mr. Rowland Hill that on one occasion having saved up sufficient money to buy a chest of drawers his wife appropriated the amount to purchase therewith a new bonnet. To punish her for this misappropriation of household goods Mr. Hill is described as having exclaimed on the following Sunday, "Here comes Mrs. Hill with a chest of drawers on her head." It is truly marvelous that this anecdote should have lived even for an hour, for Mr. Hill was of honorable family, and possessed considerable property. The purchase of any number of chests of drawers or bonnets would have been a matter of small consequence to him; and besides, he was so attached to his wife, and a man of such excellent breeding, that no such language could have been used by him under any supposable circumstances. When Mr. Hill heard of the story he said, "It is an abominable untruth, derogatory to my character as a Christian and a gentleman: it would make me out a bear." Across many of the stories which were printed concerning himself he wrote with his own hands the words, "A lie;" and truly there are others of us who might wear out our pencils in doing the same. What need is there of all this invention? We have faults enough without imputing to us more than we have committed. Men who are really eccentric furnish quite enough remarkable and singular incidents in the course of their lives, and if the actual singularities were criticized there would be no room for complaint; but wherefore all this delight in lies?

A minister who is much before the public has need to be thick skinned, and to exercise to a very high degree the virtue of longsuffering. It may help him if he will remember the conduct of good Cotton Mather, a man remarkable for the sweetness of his temper. On one occasion, having taken a prominent interest in the political concerns of his country, he received a large number of abusive letters. All of these he tied up in a packet, and wrote upon the cover, "Libels. Father, forgive them." No man of God need be astonished at slander, as though some strange thing had happened unto him, for the best servants of God have been subject to that trial. Mr. Whitefield truly said, "Thousands of prayers are put up for us, and thousands of lies are spread abroad against us." Of himself, concerning his tour in Scotland, they said, "Wherever he went he had a gaping crowd around him, and had the address to make them part with their money. He was a pickpocket, and went off to England with a full purse, but with a ruined reputation among all except his bigoted admirers." This was falsehood itself.

I commend to young preachers when they are tried in this fashion the wise and weighty words of Thomas A'Kempis:—

> "My son, take it not grievously if some think ill of thee, and speak that which thou wouldest not willingly hear.
>
> "Thou oughtest to be the hardest judge of thyself and to think no man weaker than thyself.
>
> "If thou dost walk spiritually, thou wilt not much weigh fleeting words.
>
> "It is no small wisdom to keep silence in an evil time, and in thy heart to turn thyself to God, and not to be troubled by the judgment of men.
>
> "Let not thy peace depend on the tongues of men; for whether they judge well of thee or ill, thou art not on that account other than thyself. Where are true peace and true

glory? Are they not in God? And he that careth not to please men, nor feareth to displease them, shall enjoy much peace.

"From inordinate love and vain fear ariseth all disquietness of heart and distraction of the mind."

Dr. Campbell once told me the following story:—On one occasion, when Mr. Wesley was preaching, he said, "I have been falsely charged with every crime of which a human being is capable, except that of drunkenness." He had scarcely uttered these words before a wretched woman started up and screamed out at the top of her voice, "You old villain, and will you deny it? Did you not pledge your bands last night for a noggin of whisky, and did not the woman sell them to our parson's wife?" Having delivered herself of this abominable calumny the virago sat down amid a thunder-struck assembly, whereupon Mr. Wesley lifted his hands to heaven, and thanked God that his cup was now full, for they had said *all* manner of evil against him falsely for Christ's namesake. After this we feel reconciled to the idle tales which buzz about us, annoying us for a small moment, but doing no great damage.

I would fain hope that some untruthful representations of good men are the accidental results of mis-reports. In these days when reporters must furnish brief accounts of public speeches, it is almost impossible for them to do the speakers justice, for in their hurry they hear inaccurately, and in their brevity they give of necessity but a partial report. Now, the omission of a single sentence may make a speaker appear very absurd and eccentric. Of this we have a notable instance in the case of our beloved friend Mr. C. A. Davis, of Bradford. His is a sweet, poetical, well-balanced mind, and yet one would not think so from the newspaper report of a late speech at our College meeting. He is reported to have said of us, "May every hair of your head be a wax candle to light you into glory, and may you be in heaven ten minutes before the devil knows you are dead." Assuredly this looks very outrageous as it stands; but let me personally vouch for its connection. Our friend said that he wished that he was able to express his love to us, and his hearty desires for us, and that he envied the enthusiastic ingenuity of a poor Irish woman who in thanking her benefactor exclaimed, "May, etc." Now, the reporter in this case was a friend to us all, but probably the exigencies of the printing office knocked out the previous sentences, and there stood the Catholic benediction in all its exuberance. I am somewhat amused that certain papers should abuse my brother Davis for this, for he is one of the most quiet, orderly, and correct speakers that I know of, and I congratulate him upon gaining a reputation for eccentricity by mere accident.

Do you not think it very hard that some of us can never utter a playful sentence without being criticized? Often would I speak familiarly to my dear friends, and unbosom myself, as a man might in the midst of his family, but

> "A chiel's amang ye takin' notes,
> And faith he'll prent it."

This is a sore oppression to a true-hearted man who does not care to be for ever under restraint. I sympathize thoroughly with Archdeacon Tillorson when he said, "It is surely an uneasy thing to sit always in a frame, and to be perpetually on your guard; not being able to speak a careless word, or to use a negligent posture without observation and censure. Nothing but necessity, or the hope of doing more good than a man is capable of doing in a private station, can recompense the trouble and uneasiness of a more public and busy life." The injustice of the matter is that what a man does but once in a playful moment,—and what poor slave among us does not sometimes play?—is bandied around as if it were a fair specimen of his whole life. A man in a walk chases a rare butterfly, and straightway is regarded as a mere boy who wastes his time in catching flies. But is this fair? Is it not a practical lie? For my own part, I have so long lived under a glass case, that like the bees that I have seen at the Crystal Palace I go on with my work, and try to be indifferent to spectators; and when my personal habits are truthfully reported, though they really are not the concern of anybody but myself, I feel utterly indifferent about it, except in times of depression, when I sigh for a lodge in some vast wilderness, where rumors of newspaper men and interviewers might never reach me more. Would not some of our hearers be rather more eccentric than their ministers if they were hunted and reported as we are? May heaven spare them the affliction.

Here I take leave to say that there should be greater caution in believing silly stories about ministers of the gospel, and a far greater reluctance to repeat them. They have enough to bear without being made a laughingstock before the world, for matters of which they are perfectly innocent. Taken as a body, they are probably less guilty of anything *outré*, than any other set of men; in fact, they are too apt to freeze into a cold, professional propriety: and therefore it is on all accounts unwise by exaggeration and falsehood to damp exceptional fervor because it may be attended with vivacity of spirit and originality of style.

Still there have been eccentric men, and names occur to us with which the epithet is fitly connected. Who are they? I will not dwell on Robert South, a masterly preacher, some of whose pungent expressions are almost as forcible as they are ferocious. I shall do no more than mention such personages as Dean Swift and Laurence Sterne, and I shall only allude to that witty and worthy person the Reverend Sydney Smith, for these gentlemen, with all their genres, were not overdone with gospel, and would scarcely care to be mentioned in connection with the worthies whom I shall more largely speak upon. Neither will I dwell upon the eccentric persecutors who roared and raved against Methodists and revivalists from their pulpits, except that one of them deserves "honourable mention."

"Samuel Roe, a Bedfordshire clergyman in the last century, and vicar of Stoffold, in that county, was a specimen of that inconsistent, but not uncommon character, an enthusiast against enthusiasm. Without any extraordinary capacity or attainments, he might have lived without notice, and have died without remembrance, had he not signalized himself by a proposal for preventing the further growth of Methodism,—a proposal as full of genius as it was of humanity. But this amiable and benevolent man shall be heard in his own words: 'I humbly propose to the legislative powers, when it shall seem meet, to make an example of the tabernacle preachers, by enacting a law *to cut out their tongues,* as well as the tongues of all field teachers, and others who preach in houses, barns, or elsewhere, without apostolical ordination or legal authority.'" [Larwood's Book of Clerical Anecdotes.]

I shall almost entirely confine myself to good men and true, who have really edified the church of God and led sinners to repentance.

To begin at the Reformation period, I should single out first and foremost grand old Hugh Latimer. The miter upon his head did not quench either his zeal or his wit. Is there any reformer whose name strikes with such a homely sound upon the English ear as that of Latimer? We admire Cranmer and Ridley and Hooper, and the rest of them, but we love Latimer. There is something so genuine, and as we proudly say, so thoroughly English about that honest servant of God, that whether he kisses the stake in death or rebukes kings in his life, our hearts go out towards him. Yet he was not only homely, but at times so odd and quaint in his speech that for a bishop he must be regarded as very eccentric. Did he not talk of that woman who could by no means be made to sleep till she begged them to take her to the parish church, where she had so often slept the sermon through, for she felt sure she should sleep there? Did he not tell his hearers a queer story of the countryman who thought that Tenterden steeple was the cause of the Goodwin Sands? Listen to such talk as this:— "I will tell you now a pretty story of a friar to refresh you withal. A preacher of the Gray Friars preached many times, and had but one sermon at all times, which sermon was of the ten commandments. And because this friar had preached this sermon so often, one that heard it before told the friar's servant that his master was called *Friar John Ten-Commandments;* wherefore the servant showed the friar his master thereof, and advised him to preach of some other matters; for it grieved the servant to hear his master derided. Now, the friar made answer saying, 'Belike, then, thou knowest the ten commandments well, seeing thou hast heard them so many a time.' 'Yea,' said the servant, 'I warrant you.' 'Let me hear them,' saith the master.' Then he began—'Pride, covetousness, lechery,' and so numbered the deadly sins for the ten commandments. And so there be many at this time which be weary of the old gospel; they would fain hear some new things; they think themselves so perfect in the old, when they be no more skillful than this servant was in his ten commandments."

More homely still, if possible, is his talk about the various cheats of his own day:—"I will tell you of a false practice that was practiced in my country where I dwell. But I will not tell it you to teach you to do the same, but rather abhor it, for those who use such deceitfulness shall be damned world without end. I have known some that had a barren cow, and they would fain have had a great deal of money for her, therefore they go and take a calf of another cow and put it to this barren cow, and so come to the market, pretending that this cow hath brought that calf, and so they sell their barren cow six or eight shillings dearer than they should have done else. The man which bought the cow cometh home; peradventure he hath a many of children, and hath no more cattle but this cow, and thinketh he shall have some milk for his children; but when all things cometh to pass, this is a barren cow, and so this poor man is deceived. The other fellow which sold the cow thinketh himself a jolly fellow, and a wise merchant, and he is called one that can make shift for himself. But I tell thee, whosoever thou art, do so if thou list, thou shalt do it of this price; thou shalt go to the devil, and there be hanged on the fiery gallows world without end. I tell you another false deed: I know that some husbandmen go to the market with a quarter of corn. Now, they would fain sell dear the worst, as well as the best, therefore they use this policy, they go and put a strike of fine malt or corn in the bottom of their sack, then they put two strike of the worst they had, then a good strike aloft in the sack's mouth, and so they come to the market. Now, there cometh a buyer, asking, 'Sir, is this good malt?' 'I warrant you (saith he) there is no better in this town'; and so he selleth all the malt or corn for the best, when there is but two strike of the best in the sack. The man that bought it thinketh he hath good malt, he cometh home. When he putteth the malt out of the sack, the strike which was in the bottom covereth the ill malt which was in the midst, and so the good man shall never perceive the fraud till he cometh to the occupying of the corn: the other man that sold it taketh this for a policy, but it is theft afore God, and he is bound to make restitution of so much of those two strikes which were nought [and] were sold too dear. So much he ought to restore, or else he shall never come to heaven, if God be true in his word. I could tell you of another falsehood, how they make wool to weigh much, but I will not tell it you."

Fancy the flutter among the lawn sleeves if a right reverend father were to talk in that fashion in these days. "Shockingly eccentric," would be the verdict of Canterbury and Winchester, and even of Sodor and Man.

Taking a great leap and coming down to modern times, we note the great religious revival under Whitefield and Wesley, and we ask—who is the eccentric man here? The answer is that several might be so named, but among them all the chief would be John Berridge, of Everton. What a lump of quaintness that man was; but who thinks of him at the present moment without admiration? His portrait forces you to smile, and you cannot read his letters without laughing; but what a power was upon him to stir the souls of men and lead them to the Savior's feet. Mr. Thornton seriously admonished Mr. Berridge for asking in his prayer at Tottenham Court Road that the Lord would give his people no stale bread, but that which was baked in the oven that day. I fail to see the very serious impropriety of the prayer; but when Thornton says, "You once jocularly informed me that you were born with a fool's cap on; pray, my dear sir, is it not high time that it was pulled off?" I agree with the question. Still I have more sympathy with Berridge's answer—"A fool's cap is not put off so readily as a night cap; one cleaves to the head and the other to the heart. Odd things break from me as abruptly as croaking from a raven." Berridge could not have lived if he had not found a vent for his spirits in witty sayings. He would seem to have had a fine, frank soul, which acted upon its impulses without the fear of what observers might say. Yet was he ever ready to confess his fault in the direction of excessive mirth, and on one occasion he traces it to his not being in the best physical condition. This may seem very absurd, but it is not: I have known seasons when suffering from neuralgia or depression my only hope of speaking at all has been found in taking off all the brakes, and allowing my mind to have full swing. The more my head has ached the more have I indulged in humor, or I should not have been able to speak at all. Here is the passage which I referred to, it is from one of Berridge's letters: "Laughter is not found in heaven; all are too happy there to laugh; it is a disease of fallen nature, and as such infested me sorely *when sunk into the lowest stage of a nervous complaint.* It forced itself on me without provocation, and continued with such violence as quite to overwhelm me; and nothing could check it but choking it, viz.—filling my mouth with a handkerchief." Such fits were not frequent with him, although he was always radiant with smiles. I rather admire the pluck of the man that he could laugh when he was suffering so severely. The effect which the sight of Berridge produced upon the very sober mind of Andrew Fuller is well worth mentioning. He says: "I greatly admired that divine savor, which all along mingled itself with Mr. Berridge's facetiousness, and sufficiently chastened it. His conversation tended to produce a frequent, but guileless smile, accompanied with a tear of pleasure. His love to Christ appears to be intense. The visit left a strong and lasting impression on my heart of the beauty of holiness, of holiness almost matured."

When I remember that there is credible information that in the space of about twelve months some four thousand souls were brought to Christ by his preaching, and that in the region wherein he labored his name is still mentioned as that of a great saint, I feel that there was nothing in the eccentricity of Berridge of which he needed to be ashamed.

Mr. Hill, whom Berridge calls "Dear Rowley," was hard at work for his Master when the old vicar was going off the stage, and well did he carry out the old man's advice,—"Study not to be a fine preacher: Jerichos are blown down with rams' horns. Look simply unto Jesus for preaching food, and what is wanted will be given, and what is given will be blest, whether it be a barley or a wheaten loaf, a crust or a crumb. Your mouth will be a flowing stream or a fountain sealed, according as your heart is. Avoid all controversy in preaching, talking, or writing; preach nothing down but the devil, and nothing up but Jesus Christ."

With Rowland Hill we naturally associate Matthew Wilks, who kept the Tabernacle full while Mr. Hill crowded Surrey Chapel. Of both of these we hope to speak more fully further on. America in the time of her first formation produced back-woods' preachers of a rarely eccentric order, such as Jacob Gruber, William Hibbard, James Oxley, Peter Cartwright, and others of a brave fraternity of men who labored with the axe in their hands and the gospel on their ready tongues. The same country also gave us Father Taylor, the sailor preacher of Boston. However grotesque some of these men may seem we cannot but admire their readiness for service and their unconquerable courage. Think of going to a charge where the people write, "Be sure and send us a good swimmer, for he will have to cross no end of rivers." "George," said Bishop Asbury to George Roberts, "where are your clothes?" "Bishop, they are on my back." This man carried needle and thread in case of accident to his one set of garments. We cannot countenance the propensity of Cartwright for physical warfare. We trust it will remain a peculiarity confined to America for a preacher to be equally ready to fight or to preach. Some men may be all the better for being knocked down, but the knocker down will surely be all the worse. However, these members of the church militant were rough men dealing with rough men, and we are glad that we are not tempted in the direction of fisticuffs.

The Baptists among many others of lesser note have had Robert Robinson, of Cambridge, of whom Robert Hall said that he could say "what he pleased, when he pleased, and how he pleased," and John Ryland, of Northampton, whose force and naturalness sometimes carried him into eccentric regions.

Among the Methodists have sprung up William Dawson, Gideon Ousely, Squire Brooke, and others whose names will not soon be forgotten. Now, it strikes me that if we were bound to make out a short list of earnest and successful soul-winners we might be content to take the list which we have already made out. To say the least, it is remarkable that eccentricity and usefulness often go together. These wicked eccentric people, who are so frequently condemned, have nevertheless, it turns out, been among the most useful men of their times. Matthew Wilks' way of meeting objections to his whims and oddities was not a bad one. I am told that a deputation of his friends waited upon the old gentleman to expostulate with him for his irregularities of utterance; he was shocking many good people, and his advisers hoped that he would endeavor to amend. He said, "Well, gentlemen, if you have said what you have to say, I will get you to wait just a minute or two while I run up stairs." Mr. Wilks went up stairs, and brought down a long roll of paper, which he unfolded with due dignity. "Look at that." Yes, they looked at it. "Do you see the number of names?" "Yes." "Here is another roll for you. Look at this! Count those names! Here is number three, look at this! Now, gentlemen," he said, "you see all these names? Well, then, all these precious souls profess to have found the Savior and everlasting life through what you are pleased to call my whims and oddities; and if you will find a longer roll in the hands of those who have no such whims and oddities I will try and alter my ways to please you; but until then I shall certainly follow my own course." Common sense declares Mr. Wilks to have been right. We do not say that the end justifies the means, but we would venture to hint that means which have such an end need very little justifying.

Let those whose barren ministries are as proper and decorous as a row of gravestones complain of the oddities of those who bring thousands to Christ: as for us, we have no heart for fault-finding, and only wish, without imitating their eccentricity, to find out the secret of the success of these men, if by any means we might save some. Eccentric or not eccentric will be a small matter with us if men are delivered from the wrath to come and led to trust in Jesus by the word which we preach.

3
Causes of Eccentricity

WE HAVE CONTINUED TALKING about eccentric men, but we have not yet decided what it is which makes a man eccentric. Let us now come to the point. Some ministers have been reckoned eccentric simply and only because *they have been natural.* They have been themselves, and not copies of others: what was in them they have not restrained, but have given full play to all their powers. Take for instance John Berridge. Berridge was quaint by nature. In the former lecture I quoted purposely from his letters rather than from any of his sermons or didactic works, because in a letter you see a man at ease. Berridge could not help being singular, for the form of his mind led him in that direction, and his bachelor life helped to develop his idiosyncrasies. His quaintness was all his own, and you see it in his household arrangements, as, for instance, when he says to a friend: "I am glad to see you write of a visit to Everton; we have always plenty of horse provender at hand; but unless you send me notice beforehand of your coming, you will have a cold and scanty meal; for we roast only twice in the week. Let me have a line, and I will give you the same treat I always gave to Mr. Whitefield, an eighteen-penny barn-door fowl; this will neither burst you nor ruin me; half you shall have at noon with a pudding, and the rest at night. Much grace and sweet peace be with yourself and partner; and the blessing of a new heart be with your children. With many thanks, I remain your affectionate servant, J.B."

Nor is it less manifest in his hymns, even the most sober of them, as for instance in the well-known verse where he speaks of the saints in heaven and cries—

> "Ah, Lord, with feeble steps I creep,
> And sometimes sing and sometimes weep;
> But strip me of my house of clay,
> And I will sing as loud as they."

We are not likely to censure the good man for his oddities more severely than he does himself, for in another of his pieces he writes—

> "Brisk and dull in half an hour,

> Hot and cold, and sweet and sour,
> Sometimes grave at Jesus' school,
> Sometimes light and play the fool.
>
> "What a motley wretch am I,
> Full of inconsistency!
> Sure the plague is in my heart,
> Else I could not act this part."

Rowland Hill, again, was odd by nature, and though he put great constraint upon himself his oddity would break out. On one occasion he preached in Dr. Collyer's chapel at Peckham, where everything was of the most stately order. He spoke for twenty-five minutes in a strain of deepest solemnity, but at last the real man broke out, and for the next quarter of an hour quaintness came to the front. In the vestry, at the close, he observed that he had over and over again resolved to utter no expression which could excite a smile, but, said he, "I find it's of no use. Though my very life depended upon it, I could not help myself." He never went out of his way for odd and striking sayings, he even strove to avoid them, but they were natural to him, and he was not himself without them. Do we blame the man for being himself? We blame him not, but commend him. Originality is not to be censured, but encouraged. Sir Joshua Reynolds says of painters, "Few have been taught to any purpose who have not been their own teachers." It was the excellence of Gainsborough that he formed his style for himself in the fields, and not in the studios of an academy. "The methods he used for producing his effects had very much the appearance of an artist who had never learned from others the usual and regular practice belonging to the art; for still, like a man of strong intuitive perception of what was required, he found out a way of his own to accomplish his purpose." We need in the pulpit more Gainsboroughs, for we have quite enough of the academy men of this school and the other.

Cold-hearted professionals follow each other in one line, like those caterpillars which I have seen at Mentone, which make a procession head to tail in a straight line, till you half fancy it is only one single insect; but the man who serves his God with his whole heart is apt to forget his surroundings, and to fling himself so completely into his work that the whole of his nature comes into action, and even his humor, if he be possessed of that faculty, rushes into the battle.

Some men have been dubbed eccentric because *they have been more truthful than their fellows*. Exact truth-speaking is none too common in our country. Few say that they are busy and cannot see those who call on them, but they are "not at home." Writing to persons whom they hate, many begin with, "My dear sir"; and to persons for whom they have no respect they subscribe themselves, "Your obedient servant." These are only quoted as feeble specimens of genteel falsehood; but like straws they show how the wind blows. Now there are a few men who are called eccentric because they do not believe in etiquettical lying, but speak the truth whether they offend or please. A gentleman not long ago was set down as very eccentric because being asked whether the tea was to his taste, he replied that it was not, for it was very weak and nearly cold. Others had equivocated, or had expressed themselves delighted with the nauseous decoction, and none of these were set down as eccentric. The more's the pity! Where truth is thought to be eccentric, the age itself is out of gear.

Father Taylor presided at a prayer meeting among his sailor converts, and a great man from the City came in to honor the poor people with his presence and to patronize their missionary. He made a speech, in which he extolled the kindness of the wealthy Christian people of Boston in helping to build Mr. Taylor's chapel, and assisting in his support. He praised these superior people for their great consideration of poor degraded sailors; and he gave the audience a sufficient allowance of condescension to last them for the next six months at the least. As soon as the great man had finished, Mr. Taylor quietly asked, "Is there any other old sinner from up town who would like to say a word before we go on with the meeting?" The eccentricity of that expression lay in the truthfulness which thus rebuked the impertinence of the speaker.

Good Mr. Grimshaw of Haworth once displayed his eccentricity when Mr. Whitefield was preaching in his church. Whitefield in his sermon having spoken severely of those professors of the gospel who, by their loose and evil conduct, caused the ways of truth to be evil spoken of, intimated his hope that it was not necessary to enlarge much upon that topic to the congregation before him, who had long been privileged to listen to the earnest addresses of such an able and faithful preacher. Up gets Mr. Grimshaw and says in a loud voice, "Oh! sir, for God's sake, don't speak so; I pray you do not flatter them. I fear the greater part of them are going to hell with their eyes open." Very different this from the smooth-spoken flatterer who did not desire the visit of an evangelist, because such people were only fit to preach to the wicked, and he was not aware that there was one such person in his parish.

Mr. Hill once rebuked an Antinomian who was in the habit of drinking. The man replied with a knowing look, "Now, do you think, Mr. Hill, a glass of spirits will drive grace out of my heart? "No," said the faithful old gentleman, "for there is none in it." This was putting the truth pretty clearly, and for that very reason it is spoken of as eccentric.

Matthew Wilks was remarkable for hatred of the flattering terms which certain unctuous brethren would every now and then lavish upon him. "There," said he, "I have been much pleased with my people's prayers tonight. No stuff, no flattery, no speaking of me as a dear, venerable saint, until I almost go into hysterics. Saint, indeed! A poor worm! I can scarcely refrain from speaking aloud, when such language frets my ears." To a wealthy man who had headed a subscription list for an excellent institution with a very small sum, he said, "I will have nothing to do with it since you do so little for it. You have strangled the child in its birth, when you should have nourished and cherished it until you had set it upon its feet."

Now, in these cases the eccentricity lay in plain speaking, and this is an order of eccentricity of which we cannot very well have too much, if it be accompanied by sincere affection and tempered with gentleness. But of this I feel quite sure, that if any man will make up his mind that he will only say what he believes to be strictly true, he will be thought odd and eccentric before the sun goes down.

Certain preachers have been very eccentric because *they have been manly,* too manly to be hampered by the customs and manners of the period. They have broken through one and another of the rules which have been constructed for the propping up of mannikins, and have behaved themselves as men. Mr. Binney was often thought eccentric for nothing else but his boldness and freedom from pulpit affectations. Why, sirs, there are places where it would be eccentric to speak so as to startle the drowsy; eccentric to illustrate your words by suitable action; eccentric to use a simple illustration: in fact, eccentric to utter anything more striking than the polished nullities of Blair. True-hearted men are not readily held in by the cramping-irons of childish fashion, but they are of the mind of Matthew Wilks who said, "Flesh will cry out, 'What will men say?' but a sanctified conscience will cry, 'What will God say?'" Egyptian art was reduced to an unvarying ugliness by laws which fixed the form of every feature and limb of its statues: the artist who should have anticipated the graceful life of Grecian sculpture would have been condemned by his nation as grievously eccentric, and yet unbiased ages would have exonerated the innovator from any fault; the case is the same with preachers who break through artificial rules, and boldly refuse to be mere copyists of the regulation patterns. In some places the style has been fixed by some venerated pastor who has gone to his rest; his threadbare mantle, which was excellent wear for him, is supposed to be the exact garment for his successor, and the old women of both sexes cry out against any who choose to wear their own clothes.

It is easy enough among Dissenters to find regulations as rigid as could be invented by any bench of bishops; you may not vary the length of the hymn or the order of the service by a hair's breadth, or you will sin against your own reputation and the feelings of the conservative portion of the congregation. There are few of such places now, but quite enough and, where the evil rules, the good folks are as tenacious of their established nonsense as ever the Church of England can be of her printed prayers and rubrics; and the preacher must submit to all the regular fudge as if it were Scripture itself, or be pronounced eccentric and wanting in decorum. A man that *is* a man will yield for peace sake as far as his soul is unhampered, but beyond that he will ask, "Who makes these regulations, and to what end are they made?" Finding them to be worthless and injurious, he will put his foot through them, and there will be an end of the rubbish. Some congregations are dying of dignity, and must be aroused by real life. People said that Mr. Hill rode on the back of order and decorum, and therefore he called his two horses by those names, so that if he could not ride on the back of them he might make the saying nearly true by being dragged behind them. Order and decorum, in some of our churches, have manifested themselves to be deadly sins; dead and burying the dead. Some congregations are so very orderly that they are like a vault in which the corpses lie, each one in due place, and none dares to move or lift a voice loud enough to be called a chirp. This will not do. Bring the trumpet! Sound a blast and wake the sleepers! Eccentric! Yes, eccentricity, if you like to call life by that name. Heaven knows it is sadly wanted.

After all, the eccentricities of manly life never equal those of the wretched dance (death, or sleep of death, which is so dear to mere routine. Think of such an event as the following happening among your orderly readers of other men's discourses, for the like has happened and must have happened many times. A certain preacher delivered a discourse in which occurred such a passage as this: "On account of your sins, and your neglect of the house of God, your wantonness and your gluttony, the anger of the Most High is provoked, and therefore is this great plague come upon you, and death is raging in every street." When the sermon was finished the officials of the township came to know where this plague was, and what deaths had happened; indeed, all the congregation were anxious to know where this dreadful disease was raging. "Oh," said this orderly reader of sermons, "I do not know where it is, but it was in my sermon, and so I was obliged to read it to you." It would be easy enough to on. large upon the accidents which must occur where borrowed, or rather stolen, sermons are preached; but this is not my point, I merely mention this as one instance of the way in which prosy routine becomes itself ludicrous. To me it seems always ludicrous if looked at through the glass of truth. Primness, fashionableness, and dignity are but little separated from the ridiculous; at their very best there is but one step between them, and that step is often taken with grave obliviousness that it is so.

I make bold to say that some men have been styled eccentric because *they are really in earnest,* and earnestness defies rules. I do not believe that it is possible for a man in downright earnest to be always "proper." I suppose there is a proper way of getting a lady out of her bedchamber when her house is on fire, but doubtless our firemen often violate the proprieties when they have such a thing to do. They have to rush in anyhow to save life, and they cannot stay to make apologies. The flames are urgent, and so must the rescuer be, or life will be lost. I suppose there is a proper way of pulling persons out of the water when they are drowning, but I have known brave fellows drag them out by the hair of their heads: this was rough and rude, but it answered the purpose. Did any one ever blame the doer of the deed for his roughness? Is not the soul more precious than the body, and who would suffer it to be lost for the sake of etiquette? A man may go into the pulpit as prim as you please, and he may even wear tight-fitting lavender gloves, such as I have heard of; but let him feel an inward anguish for the souls of men and he will forget his dignity and burst his gloves, and in all probability never buy a second pair. A man may be stiffly proper, and even elegant and delicate till he comes to real grips with men's consciences, and then, like the soldier at Waterloo who wished to be in his shirt-sleeves, he will feel hampered by his buckram and his starch, and speak like a man to men, and then some booby or other will hold up his hands and cry, "Dear me, how dreadfully eccentric!"

A few divines have seemed to be eccentric because of *the wealth of poetry which dwelt in their speech.* Men of the prosaic school are quite startled by expressions which to poetical minds are natural enough, and by no means singular. It needs genius in the hearer to enjoy genius in the preacher. One of my personal friends, whose sermons are essentially poems, laughed the other day right heartily at the expression of an admiring hearer, who did not at one time appreciate him. "Ah," said the good man, "I am very sorry that I was so foolish as to leave your ministry for a time; but then, you see, *I used to hear you with a jaundiced eye!*" It is this jaundiced eye of cold matter-of-fact which is unable to perceive the beauty of sparkling metaphors and images, and therefore sees instead mere eccentricity. In my earlier days I have heard rustic prayers which thrilled *me,* not only with their spirituality, but with their poetry, and yet I heard others exclaiming against the extravagance of the language. One whom many regarded as eccentric in his preaching was a great favorite with me, and I remember now his striking sayings, his choice aphorisms, and his rare imagery, while other sermons have faded from my memory, because they never touched my heart. I could have said of him what John Bradford said of Latimer, "I have an ear for other divines, but I have a heart for you." Doubtless there are many others who are condemned for their eccentricity by the simpletons around them, because they have wealthy creative minds, and scatter pearls with both their hands.

Eccentricity has also been charged on *men of shrewd common sense.* They have baffled those who sought to entrap them, and, in revenge, their adversaries have dubbed them eccentric. They were not quite so easily gulled as their contemporaries, but leveled a little mother-wit at cants, and hypocrites, and deriders, and so they must be libeled as odd fellows. As this is a point which I do not intend to dwell upon at any length, I will only illustrate it by the story of the eccentric shepherd, and remark that similar shrewdness on the part of ministers is of the utmost value, but is pretty sure to incur the charge of eccentricity. Here is the story. "An exceedingly proud clergyman, riding over a common, saw a shepherd tending his flock, and wearing a new coat. The parson asked in a haughty tone who gave him that coat. 'The same people (said the shepherd) that clothe you—the parish.' The clergyman, nettled a little, rode on murmuring a considerable way, and at length sent his man back to ask the shepherd if he would come and live with him, for he thought of keeping a fool. The man went to the shepherd accordingly and delivered his master's message, imagining that his master really wanted a fool. 'Are *you* going away then?' said the shepherd. 'No,' answered the other. 'Then you may tell your master (replied the shepherd) that his living won't maintain *three* of us.'" Such crushing replies Rowland Hill and others were quite capable of giving to hypocrites and mockers, and they did well thus to silence them, but it earned them the title of eccentric.

Some men have been eccentric on account of *the vast amount of dramatic energy with which they have been endowed,* Certain persons when they talk suit the action to the word from the force of nature and habit. It is in their way to be dramatic. Look at a Frenchman, how he speaks with his hands, his shoulders, his eyebrows, his feet, and his whole body. Very few Englishmen are thus dramatic, but here and there we meet with persons who are as energetic in that direction as the liveliest of our Gallic neighbors. And why not? The famous William, or as the public delighted to say, *"Billy,"* Dawson, was nothing if not dramatic. I have heard a wellknown minister tell that Dawson was once preaching about Noah's ark, and finding himself boxed up in the pulpit he said, "This won't do." He opened the pulpit door and he came down the stairs to the bottom of the pulpit, and there he began to fell trees and cut and saw them, and then he seemed to be hammering away to make the ark, which was represented by the pulpit. This ark was made before them all, the people being worked up to an extreme excitement while Dawson continued to cry, "There is a flood coming, I am making this ark for the saving of my house; there is no hope for anybody but those who come into the ark." Then he seemed to be boiling a great cauldron of pitch, until he took his long brush and pitched the ark within and without, and when all was done there was his ship on the dry land, and like Noah he turned round and asked the people once again whether they would come into it and be saved. They would not come in, and so he declared he would go in alone. He went up into the pulpit and shut the door with the words, "And the Lord shut him in." Then came the flood, and our informant said that he felt as if the floor of the chapel burst up and the water began bubbling from below, while great water-floods poured from above in mighty torrents; and there was Dawson, another Noah, all alive and safe, crying out that it was now too late, for the door was shut. All were awed and filled with breathless attention while he bade them remember that such would soon be the case, and preached unto them Jesus as the only salvation. None of us would attempt this, but I would not have laid a finger on Dawson. Why should he not depict the scene in his own way? If God gave him the histrionic faculty, why should he not use it to impress his hearers? Perhaps he knew that those who were around him could not be impressed in any other way. This was he who on another occasion described David and Goliath. He represented David coming forth with his sling, and the giant boasting that he would give his flesh to the fowls of the air and to the beasts of the field, and so on; but David replies, "Thou comest to me with a sword, and with a spear, and with a shield; but I come to thee in the name of the Lord of hosts." He laid his stone carefully in the sling, whirled the sling in the air, and you could hear the stone whizzing towards the giant's brow. Just then Sammy Hick, the village blacksmith, who was sitting near the preacher, rose up under tremendous excitement and cried, "Now then, Billy, off with his head.!"

For my part, I like this dramatizing kept within check and thoroughly well done. You have, probably, seen Mr. Gough do that sort of thing admirably in his orations. Have I not seen him walk what seemed to me miles while he was delivering one of his addresses, rushing over the plains and through the rivers, and at last up the sides of Vesuvius after a bubble? I think I see him now, with his feet sinking in the hot ashes, struggling in vain and perishing before our eyes. It was grandly done, and no one had a right to object to it. Gough has caught Garrick's idea, and speaks of truths as truths, making them visible before our eyes. I know the criticisms which are so easy to make about histrionic displays, theatrical action, miracle plays, and so forth, and I know also the real dangers which surround the practice; but I would far rather incur all the supposable perils than altogether banish such an awakening force from the pulpit.

Sometimes men have been regarded as eccentric because *they have been practical*. The occasion has demanded what in other circumstances would have been unjustifiable, and others not knowing the peculiar conditions have set their words and actions in another light, and made them seem objectionable. They meant to save men's souls somehow, by the blessing of God, and therefore they resolved to do anything and everything by which they could get at the stolid, ignorant, and indifferent; and hence the things which they did have been *outré* and striking, but not more so than the need required. Such singular words or acts have been divorced from the circumstances out of which they grew, and put aside from the connection; the design of the preacher has been forgotten, and then the thing which has been done has seemed to be eccentric at least, if not censurable; though, mark you, had you yourself been there, and had you possessed the preacher's ready wit and intense earnestness, you could scarcely have done better. Let me give you one or two instances, and the first is from Mr. Grant's sketch of Rowland Hill in "The Metropolitan Pulpit"; it is told in a somewhat wordy style, but the change from my more abrupt manner may be a relief:—"A pious woman, a member of Surrey Chapel, was married to a husband who, though kind to her, had no sense of religion, but delighted in spending the hours in swilling beer which she spent in attendance on the preaching of the gospel. It so happened that the couple, through some disappointment in business, had been unable to pay their rent on a particular quarter day. The consequence was that a distraint on their furniture was put into their house, and a party was employed, as the technical phrase has it, 'to take possession.' After turning over every scheme in their minds which could suggest itself for extricating themselves from the difficulties in which they were involved, they were about to despair, when the idea occurred to the wife of submitting the circumstances of the case to Mr. Hill. She accordingly proceeded to his house, at once got access to him, and with no small degree of tremor made a short and simple representation of the state of matters.

"'How much would you require to save your furniture and get rid of the person in possession?' enquired Mr. Hill.

"'Eighteen pounds, sir, would be quite sufficient for the purpose,' answered the poor woman, with a palpitating heart.

"'I'll let you have the loan of twenty, and you can repay me at your convenience. Send your husband to me on your return home, and I will have two ten pound notes ready by the time he arrives. I wish to give the notes to him rather than to you.'

"Mrs. D—quitted Mr. Hill's house and hurried home with light foot, but with a still lighter heart. Having communicated to her husband what had passed between herself and her minister, it is unnecessary to say that he lost no time in proceeding to the house of Mr. Hill. The latter received him with much kindness of manner.

"'And so,' said he, 'you are so unfortunate as to have a person in possession.'

"'We unfortunately have, sir.'

"'And twenty pounds will be sufficient to get rid of him and restore your furniture to you?'

"'It will, sir.'

"'Well, then,' said Mr. Hill, pointing to the table, 'there are two ten pound notes for you, which you can repay when you are able. Take them.'

"The other advanced to the table, took the notes, and was in the act of folding them up, at the same time warmly thanking Mr. Hill for the act of friendship he had done him, and expressing a hope that he would soon be able to pay the amount back again, when the reverend gentleman suddenly exclaimed, 'Stop a little! Just lay the notes down again until I ask a blessing on them.'

"The other did as he was desired, on which Mr. Hill, extending both his arms, uttered a short prayer to this effect:—' O Lord, who art the

Author of all mercy and the Giver of every good and perfect gift, do thou be graciously pleased to bless the sum of money which is given to him who is now before thee, that it may conduce to his present and eternal welfare. For Jesus Christ's sake."

"'Now sir,' said Rowland Hill, as he finished his brief supplication, 'now, sir, you may take the money.'

"The party a second time took up the two ten pound notes, and was in the act as before of folding them up, when Mr. Hill interposed, by reminding him that he had forgotten one thing. It may be easily supposed that by this time he was a good deal confused. His confusion was increased a hundredfold when Mr. Hill remarked, 'But, my friend, you have not yourself asked for a blessing on the money. You had better do it now.'

"'Sir,' faltered out the other, scarcely able to support himself, 'sir, I cannot pray. I never prayed in all my life.'

"'You have the more need to begin now,' observed the reverend gentleman, in his own cool yet rebuking manner.

"'I cannot, sir; I do not know what to say.'

"'Try, try and thank God and ask his blessing, however short your prayer may be.'

"'I cannot, sir;! cannot say a single sentence.'

"'Then you can't have the money. I will not lend twenty pounds to a prayer-less man.'

"The other hesitated for a moment, and then with dosed eyes, and uplifted hands, he said with great earnestness, 'O Lord, what shall I say to thee and to Mr. Hill on this occasion?' He was about to begin another sentence, when the reverend gentleman interrupted him by observing,' That will do for a beginning. It is a very excellent first prayer, for it is from the heart. Take the money, and may God's blessing be given along with it.' As he spoke, Mr. Hill took up the two ten pound notes, and transferring them to the half-bewildered man, cordially shook him by the hand, and wished him good morning.

"It only remains for me to mention, that not only did the husband and wife become prosperous in secular matters, but the incident made so deep an impression on the husband's mind as to end in his conversion to God."

It was strange thus as it were to drive a man to pray, but who shall say it was wrong? My second incident is more wild, and I give it as I recollect it; if I err in accuracy I shall be sorry, but I will tell it as nearly as I remember it. A Methodist preacher went to a certain town in the north, but found hardly anyone to hear him, and he preached a while with no stir appearing among the dry bones. One Sunday morning he said, "I tell you what it is, friends. This town is responsible to God for the possession of the means of grace, which it does not use. I cannot get the people to hear, but I can remove some of their responsibility by destroying the pulpit which they despise, and the place of worship which they will not enter. Here is a beginning; we will break the desk to pieces at once, and then if no one comes we will clear out the pews and everything else, and leave the chapel a wreck. The people shall not perish with the gospel so close to them. The candlestick shall be taken away since they refuse the light." He commenced by laying his axe at the pulpit, and in part demolishing it, before the eyes of the few who were present. "Now," said he, "tell your friends that there is part of the responsibility gone, and the rest will follow." The astonished folks went home and spread the amazing news, and in a very short time the place was thronged. You say, "This *was* an eccentric man." Well, I do not justify his proceedings, but I judge that he knew his own way about better than I could have shown it to him. After all, he was only sacrificing a few boards; and at that small cost he broke through that indifference which more costly methods might have failed to touch. Within a little time Methodism lifted up its head in the town, and the forlorn meeting-house rang with songs of praise. Why, dear me, if the Tabernacle were empty, and we could not fill the house without doing or saying something striking, I think we might, if it were for the first time in our life, run the risk of being thought eccentric.

Everything looks ridiculous or not according to its surroundings. Wisdom and wit may become folly and even falsehood, if they are severed from the occasion which called them forth. Listen to an ancient tale of a traveler who reported that he had seen a cabbage so large that a whole regiment of soldiers took shelter under it from a shower of rain. To him another, who was no traveler, asked if they would believe him if he told them that on the very day in which this cabbage was seen he had himself passed by a place where four hundred braziers were making a cauldron—two hundred of them hammering outside, and two hundred inside fastening the rivets! The traveler eagerly inquired of what use such a cauldron could be, and received the following answer. "Sir, it was to boil your cabbage.":Now, if this second person's story was repeated away from its connection, and its form slightly altered, a richly deserved rebuke would be made to look like an attempt to exceed in lying. Many a word spoken or the principle of answering a fool according to his folly has been quoted against a wise man, and the folly has been laid at the wrong door.

There is an extraordinary story of Father Andre, a French preacher of great repute, for what was called eccentricity. He was preaching one afternoon to a congregation or persons who disregarded re-Jigion both as to themselves and their families, and he wished both to convict them and to upbraid them for the bad way in which they were bringing up their little ones. He first asked the children questions from the Catechism, and obtained no replies; and he then shook his sleeve, and out there flew a pack of cards. The people were shocked with him, of course, but he quietly looked down and said to one of the children, "Boy, bring me a card. You boy, bring me another. You girl, another, and come here with them!" They gathered around the pulpit, and he asked of one, "What is this card, my child?" The boy answered at once. The next, a girl, came up, and she also knew her card. He continued his questions till he had gone far into the pack, and received correct answers all round. "Ah," he says, "I see how you are training your children. You teach them to know all the cards, but you do not instruct them in the faith. Are you not ashamed of yourselves?" Here I pronounce no verdict, I could not have done it myself, nor should I like to hear of any friend of mine doing the like; but I cannot tell what was good for Catholics in France so long ago.

Lassenius, a Dutch court preacher, in the end of the seventeenth century, had been greatly vexed by seeing a considerable part of his congregation going to sleep. One day he suddenly stopped, and pulling out a battledore and shuttlecock, began playing with them. Of course, the sleepers all awoke directly; the wakeful ones jogging their neighbors to share in their astonishment. Then Lassenius turned upon them with a severe rebuke. "When I announce to you serious and important truths, you are not ashamed to go to sleep; but when I play the fool you are all eye and ear." Sharp medicine this for a desperate disease, and the physician who administered it was in grievous danger of injuring himself. I do not think that I can justify this procedure, but I do not know the Dutch people so well as Lassenius did, and my own people never go to sleep, and so I do not pretend to form an opinion one way or the other. Certainly it must, be very provoking to see people sleeping, and yet it is not so very wonderful that they should do so when we consider the drowsy sounds to which they are doomed to listen. "I feel very tired with preaching," said a young bombastic preacher. "O man," said a shrewd old hearer, "did you say you were tired?

If you are only half as tired of it as I am, I pity you." I am afraid that this side of the question is too often forgotten.

The following story is worth recording. I do not hesitate to say that I should have done the same, and should have felt justified in thus practically rebuking a miserable people for leaving their place of worship in such a shameful condition.

"The Rev. Zabeliel Adams at one time exchanged with a neighboring minister—a mild, inoffensive man—who knowing the peculiar bluntness of his character, said to him,' You will find some panes of glass broken in/he pulpit window, and possibly you may suffer from the cold. The cushion, too, is in a bad condition; but I beg of you not to say anything to my people on the subject; they are poor, and sensitive!' 'O no! O no!' said Mr. Adams, 'You may trust me to be very quiet about such things.' But ere he left home he filled a bag with rags and took it with him. When he had been in the pulpit a short time, feeling somewhat in-commoded by the free circulation of the air, he deliberately took from the bag a handful of rags, and stuffed them into the windows. Towards the close of his discourse, which was more or less upon the duties of a people towards their minister, he became very animated, and purposely brought down both fists upon the pulpit cushion with tremendous force. The feathers flew in all directions, and the cushion was nearly emptied. He checked the current of his thoughts, and simply exclaimed, 'Why, how these feathers fly!' and then proceeded. He had fulfilled his promise of not addressing the people on the subject, but had taught them a lesson not to be misunderstood. On the next Sabbath the window anti cushion were found in excellent repair."

I have talked to you thus cheerfully about eccentric preachers, but I would not have you forget the serious side of the matter. If I were addressing a congregation I would say to them,—If you knew how we desire to lay hold of your minds for Christ, and how willingly we would be as solemn as death itself if we thought that this would win your hearts, you would not so much blame our occasional sallies. If you knew how little we desire notoriety, and how much we desire to save your souls, you would commend our object and excuse our style. We ramble because you ramble. O that we could seize the wandering sheep, and bring them home to the true fold. I say, if you knew the desire we have to bring men to Christ, you would not be so ready to catch at every little thing which violates the canons of taste. Besides, we are not bound to abide by your judgments. May it not be possible that we know what we are at as well as you do? Will you take our work and do it better? If so, we are ready to learn by your example.

Judge the preacher if you like, but do remember that there is something better to be done than that, namely, to get all the good you can out of him, and pray his Master to put more good into him. What if the man be odd and strange, yet, as men take pearls out of oyster shells, so may you be willing to accept from God whatever of precious truth he sends you. Despise not the heavenly treasure because of the earthen vessel. Lose not an opportunity of being enriched because the gold lies in connection with common earth.

And, oh, dear brothers, who are engaged in winning souls, let me say to you, by the memories of all these good men who have gone before you, and who were counted eccentric, fear no man's frown, and court no man's smile, but say the right thing and the true, and say it as best you can, and ask God's help that you may say it so that you may make men feel it, even though you sting them into anger; for blessed shall that man be who has discharged his conscience before the living God. Do not sacrifice your hearers' souls to your own reputations. Be fools for Christ's sake, if need be, that you may gain the careless ones. The curse of the age is the unearthly ministry which mocks it. I say "unearthly," but I do not mean heavenly, I mean unpractical, unhuman,—a thing which does not come home to men, or arouse the slightest interest in their minds. Do you believe that our working men would, as a rule, shun the churches of London if they were there regaled with hearty, homely discourses such as they could understand, and such as would touch their every-day life? I, for one, have reason to speak to the contrary, and that without a shadow of a doubt. Do you think that England would be so ready to be enticed back to Rome if all her ministers were preaching the gospel as they ought to be? With such a company of preachers discoursing twice every Sunday, besides the weekday exercises, ought not our island to be illuminated, as by the sun at noon, so that it would be impossible for the Roman darkness to return. Things would have been very different if there had been more love, more earnestness, more passion for souls in the pulpit; but then I greatly fear that there would also have been more eccentric men. Do you dread the evil? I share not your fear, but say, God send it, so that is be an outgrowth of true life.

4
Hugh Latimer, 1480—1555

POPISH HISTORIANS HAVE NOT hesitated to describe Latimer as extremely eccentric. Lingard says, "His eloquence was bold and vehement, but poured forth in coarse and sarcastic language, and seasoned with quaint low jests and buffoonery." This accusation is evidently made for the purpose of whitewashing Popery and blackening the Reformation. It is with pleasure that we read it, because it enables us to entail the bishop amongst the noble army of the slandered servants of God. We have no wish to deny that Latimer was exceedingly quaint, and intermingled flashes of pleasantry with his earliest exhortations and serious arguments; but it was always with the view of confounding error and reaching the hearts of his hearers.

Here is an example of his shrewdness. Dr. Buckingham, one of the Black Friars, undertook to confute Latimer, and in his sermon said among other remarkably wise things that the reading of the Scriptures in the vulgar tongue would cause people to leave their vocations, and run into all sorts of extremes. "Thus," said he, "for example, the ploughman, when he heareth this in the gospel, 'no man that layeth his hand on the plough and looketh back is meet for the kingdom of God,' will peradventure upon this cease from his ploughing. Likewise the baker, when he heareth that 'a little leaven corrupteth the whole lump of dough,' may perchance leave our bread unleavened, and so our bodies be unseasoned." Latimer heard this sermon, and engaged to answer the arguments, which he did from the same pulpit in the afternoon, Dr. Buckingham sitting opposite to him with his Black Friars' cowl upon his shoulders. After discoursing upon the figurative phrases of Scripture, Latimer said that such metaphors were commonly used and were well understood in all languages, "as for example," observed he, looking towards the place where the friar sat, "when the painters represent a fox preaching out of a friar's cowl, no one is so weak as to take this for a real fox, but only as a figure of caution to beware of that hypocrisy, craft, and dissimulation which lie hid many times under those cowls."

The general preaching of Latimer before and after he became a bishop was very plain and homely, and exactly suited to the manners and tastes of the people to whom he spoke. His sermons should be read by every lover of racy English. We have only space for one extract, which will show how very plain and colloquial he could be. "A good fellow on a time had another of his friends to a breakfast, and said, If you will come, you shall be welcome; but I tell you aforehand, you shall have but slender fare, one dish, and that is all. What is that? said he. A pudding, and nothing else. Marry (said he), you cannot please me better; of all meats, this is for mine own tooth; you may draw me round about the town with a pudding. These bribing magistrates and judges follow gifts faster than the fellow would follow the pudding." Latimer wanted his words to be remembered so as to work reform, and he did well to put them in such a shape that they would ring over the land. We will warrant that this pudding story of his did more for justice than a dozen refined orations. His was practical preaching, and it dealt with the sins of the great as well as with those of the common people, in tones too honest to be very polite.

The dauntless courage of this noble servant of God was seen in his conduct towards Henry VIII. One new year's day, instead of carrying, according to the custom of that age, a rich gift to the king, he presented him with the New Testament, a leaf of which was turned down at this passage, "Whoremongers and adulterers God will judge." This might have cost him his life; but bluff Hal, instead of being angry, admired the good man's courage. Upon a certain occasion, when preaching before Henry, Hugh, as was his wont, spake his mind very plainly, and the sermon displeased his majesty; he was therefore commanded to preach again on the next Sabbath, and to make an apology for the offense he had given. After reading his text, the bishop thus began his sermon:—"Hugh Latimer, dost thou know before whom thou art this day to speak? To the high and mighty monarch, the king's most excellent majesty, who can take away thy life if thou offendest; therefore take heed that thou speakest not a word that may displease! But then consider well, Hugh, dost thou not know from whence thou comest; upon whose message thou art sent? Even by the great and mighty God! who is all present! and who beholdeth all thy ways! and who is able to cast thy soul into hell! Therefore, take care that thou deliverest thy message faithfully." He then proceeded with the same sermon he had preached the preceding Sabbath, but with considerably more energy. The sermon ended, the court were full of expectation to know what would be the fate of this honest and plain-dealing bishop. After dinner, the king called for Latimer, and with a stern countenance asked him how he durst preach in such a manner. He, falling on his knees, replied, his duty to his God and his prince had enforced him thereto, and that he had merely discharged his duty and cleared his conscience by what he had spoken.

Upon which the king, rising from his seat, and taking the good man by the hand, embraced him, swing, "Blessed be God, I have so honest a servant."

Under Edward VI. Latimer had great influence, but the return of Mary soon called him to severer conflicts. Dauntless, honest, and simple-hearted, Latimer rejoiced when he was called upon to lay down his bishopric; and when he was summoned to be tried for his life the old man hesitated not to appear and defend our holy faith to the death. His words at the stake were characteristic of the man. Addressing Bishop Ridley, who was to die with him, he said, "Be of good comfort, Master Ridley, and play the man. We shall this day light such a candle by God's grace in England as I trust shall never be put out." *And by God's grace it never shall be.*

5
Hugh Peters, 1599—1660

THE MOST SLANDERED MAN of his times was Hugh Peters, who was executed at the Restoration as a ringleader in the so-called Great Rebellion. He is usually set down as a wretched jester, and traduced as a mountebank, whereas there is far more evidence to show that he was a zealous preacher of the gospel. We give him a place here, not because we altogether admire him, but as a matter of justice to one who has been falsely accused.

In his unconverted life he was a daring sinner; but after he was converted he became a powerful preacher of the word. At St. Sepulchre's Church his preaching was very popular, and, better still, it was made useful in the conversion of hundreds. Having in a prayer for the queen uttered words which were taken to imply that she was in need of repentance, as in all probability she was, he was imprisoned by Laud. He ultimately fled the country, and became a pastor, first in Holland, and then in America. His reputation was so great that his brother colonists sent him home as a mediator upon important business. Here he was detained by the breaking out of the civil wars, during which he became an army chaplain, was present at many great battles, and was frequently sent up to the parliament to report progress.

Peters was at one time secretary to Oliver Cromwell. Carlyle quotes his description of the taking of Basing House, and speaks of him as "a man concerning whom the reader has heard so many falsehoods." The utmost malice of the Cavaliers was expended in blackening this man's character with the view of excusing his execution by Charles II., which was nothing better than a judicial murder. A respectable biographer says of him, "Peters was not a wise man in all things; he was forward and hasty of speech, but he was a true and sincere man; a man of unblemished reputation in circles where nothing foul or mean was tolerated, and a man who in every respect was immensely the superior of those who traduced him.

It was the common expression of those days that the saints should have the praises of God in their mouths and a two-edged sword in their hands, and this was far too prominently the case with Peters. He was "the fighting parson" of his day; but like the Ironsides among whom he ministered he was a devout soldier, and was made a soldier by his devotion. Our views and sympathies do not run in that direction, but we are too much indebted to the warriors of the Commonwealth to be in a hurry to condemn them. There was an intense earnestness about Hugh Peters, and as his sermons were meant for soldiers, and had relation to stormy politics, they were in all probability rough-hewn, and by no means pleasant in the ears of cavaliers; but the coarse jests which were imputed to him were evidently none of his, since they were current long before he was born. Some studious owner of the little volume in the British Museum which records these vile witticisms has annotated it in such a way as to prove that the larger number of the anecdotes are fabrications. Thus, "Jest 1: This is a Norman tale of the twelfth or thirteenth century. Jest 14: Taken from Taylor, the water poet's works," etc.

Nevertheless, such stories as the following may have some truth in them: "Praying in a village, he espied in the church the king's arms, whereupon he brought in these words, *Good Lord, keep us from the yoke of tyranny;* and spreading his hands towards the king's arms, saith he, *Preserve thy servants from the paw of the lion and the horn of the unicorn.*

"Discoursing of the advantage Christians have above heathens, and showing that the heathen are guided by a natural instinct, but we have the word preached to us; and indeed, saith he, the gospel hath a very free passage amongst us, for I am confident it no sooner enters in at one ear, but it is out at the other.

"Mr. Peters espying a friend of his, deeply cut in the head, through having engaged in a foolish fray, he began to check him for his indiscretion. But, saith he, 'tis too late now to give you counsel; come along with me to a surgeon, and I'll see you drest. Where being come, the surgeon begun to wash away the blood, and search for his brains, to see if they were hurt. At which Mr. Peters cries out,' What a mad man are you to seek for any such thing; if he had possessed any brains he would never have ventured into so foolish a contest.'"

Hugh Peters sinned against the whole party of Church-and-King by his zealous defense of the Parliamentary cause, and at the same time he shocked the Presbyterians by pleading for A TOLERATION OF ALL SECTS, and this was reckoned to be the very worst of crimes. Men who are in advance of their age are abused for principles which in due time become accepted. A man who was secretary to Oliver Cromwell, who had Philip Nye and Goodwin for intimate friends, and Milton for his apologist, was not a bad man: this is morally certain. His peculiarities arose out of his passionate enthusiasm for the cause of liberty, and the remarkable combination in his person of soldier and preacher.

In the works of Hugh Peters there are no indications of his being a jester, but abundant evidence of his genius and fertility of mind. The little book entitled "A Dying Father's Last Legacy to an only Child" was written by his own hand just before his execution, and is rich in holy instruction. Here are extracts:—

"He that sets up religion to get anything by it more than the glory of God and the saving his own soul will make a bad bargain of it at the close."

"Make Christ your wisdom. Oh that you were thus wise! Much of wit must be pared off before it will be useful. I have seen the ways of it though I never could pretend to much of it: but this I know, that being unsanctified, wit is a sword in a madman's hand. It spends itself in vanity, foolish jesting, and abuse of those who are weaker than ourselves, yea, it often leads men to play with the blessed word of God."

"If I go shortly where time shall be no more, where neither cock nor clock distinguishes hours, sink not, but lay thy head in his bosom who can keep thee, for he sits upon the waves."

6
Daniel Burgess, 1645—1713

THE NAME OF DANIEL Burgess is usually associated with jesting, but this is another instance of the way in which worthy men have been held up to ridicule. He was a Dissenter, and a man of great courage and boldness of speech; he was also a quaint and attractive preacher, and so the word went forth from the evil one that he should be denounced as a buffoon. In those days there was no law to protect the Dissenter, or at least no officer who cared to put it in force, and so Mr. Burgess and his congregation were shamefully annoyed by persons of the baser sort; but when he was urged to prosecute these disturbers he only replied, "No, I have freely forgiven them, and shall never meditate revenge." These are not the words of a buffoon.

His hearers procured for him a meeting-house in Brydges Street, Covent Garden, where a large congregation always gathered. "Being situated," says one of his biographers, "in the neighborhood of the theater, and surrounded by many who were fools enough to mock at sin and religion, he frequently had among his hearers those who came only to make themselves merry at the expense of religion, Dissenters, and Daniel Burgess. This his undaunted courage, his pointed wit, and ready elocution turned to great advantage: for he frequently fixed his eye on those scoffers, and addressing them personally in a lively, piercing, and serious manner, was blessed to the conversion of many who came only to mock."

He continued as pastor over this congregation for thirty years, during which a new place of worship was built by them in Carey Street, and when this was utterly wrecked by Sacheverell's mob, it was repaired at the expense of the government; but the expense and trouble to which they were put seriously burdened his people. He died January 1712-13, in the sixty eighth year of his age, and was buried at St. Clement Danes, Strand. A writer says, "It has escaped the notice of his biographers, that the celebrated Lord Bolingroke was once his pupil, and the world has to regret that his lordship did not learn what Daniel Burgess might have taught him; for Daniel, with all his oddities, which made him for so many years the butt of Swift, Steele, and the other wits of the time, was a man of real piety."

One story which is told of him may have possibly been true, but we are not sure. When treating on the robe of righteousness, he said, "If any of you would have a good and cheap suit, you will go to Monmouth

Street; if you want a suit for life, you will go to the Court of Chancery; but if you wish for a suit that will last to eternity, you must go to the Lord Jesus Christ, and put on his robe of righteousness." This is probably a garbled quotation. The reader may accept it *cum grano salis*.

Although it pleased the graceless wit-lings of his day to father silly stories upon Burgess, it is clear to all impartial persons that he was a man of mark, and of deep piety. When the Society for the Reformation of Manners was instituted he was selected to preach the first sermon. This was published under the title of "The Golden Snuffing," aria is a proof of how the good man was vilified; for a critic describes it as "replete with forced puns," and we therefore procured it, but cannot find a pun in it, and scarcely anything quotable for special quaintness,,unless it be the following passage: "Christ's ministers are your souls' physicians. We are not fiddlers to tickle your ears, nor confectioners to please your palates, but physicians to cure your diseases, and if you nauseate our most needful medicines we dare not withhold them, and gratify you with sugared poisons." We are sure that the critic never saw the sermon, but judged it from the title alone. The first choice of the preacher by a society which commanded the ablest ministers would not have fallen on a mere buffoon.

Our best evidence that Daniel Burgess was a good man and true is found in the facts that he was thought worthy by his contemporaries to preach one of the sermons in the famous series of "Morning Exercises," that he was much beloved by the excellent Dr. Bates, and that Matthew Henry preached a funeral sermon for him, wherein his homely speech is admitted and abundantly justified. With an extract from this sermon our brief notice must conclude:—

"He often said he chose rather to be profitable than fashionable in his preaching, and that he thought it cost him more pains to study plainness than it did others to study fineness; and he would be willing to go out of the common way to meet with sinners, to persuade them to return to their God. 'That is the best key (said he) that fits the lock, and opens the door, though it be not a silver or a golden one.' Many have acknowledged that they came to hear him at first only to scoff at him, and make a jest of what he said, but went away under such convictions about the concerns of their souls and another world, as, it was hoped, ended in a happy change of their spirits.

"In his preaching he insisted mostly upon the first great principles of religion, which all good Christians are agreed in; and one who was a very competent judge told me, he thought he had as good a faculty in demonstrating them, and making them plain and evident, as most men he ever heard. He much lamented and vigorously opposed the growth of deism and infidelity among us, saying he dreaded a 'Christless Christianity.' He meddled not with party matters, or matters of doubtful disputation, but plainly made it his aim to bring people to-believe in Jesus Christ, and to live in all godliness and honesty. He was particularly careful to explain the two covenants of works and grace, and to guard against the two rocks of presumption and despair. He now and then used some plain similitude's or surprising turns of expression, or little stories, such perhaps as we find Bishop Latimer's sermons full of, which by some were turned to his reproach; but it is certain many particular stories were maliciously fathered on him, that were abominably false, and raised by a lying spirit only to obstruct his usefulness; and in the general he was industriously misrepresented by many, who it is to be feared therein discovered no kindness for serious godliness. A gentleman having once the curiosity to go to hear him, when he had done, could scarce be made to believe that this was Mr. Burgess; for, said he, 'I never heard a better sermon in my life.!'"

7
John Berridge, 1716—1793

JOHN BERRIDGE, THE VICAR of Everton, was commended by John Wesley as one of the most simple as well as most sensible of all whom it pleased God to employ in reviving primitive Christianity. He was a man of remarkable learning, being as familiar in the learned languages as in his mother tongue, and well instructed in theology, logic, mathematics, and metaphysics: he was not, therefore, eccentric because he was ignorant. He possessed a strength of understanding, quickness of perception, depth of penetration, and brilliancy of fancy beyond most men, while a vein of innocent humor ran through all his public and private discourses. His biographer tells us that this softened what some might call the austerity of religion, and rendered his company pleasant to people of a less serious habit; and yet he adds,—"It is very singular that it never overcame his own gravity; he remained serious himself while others were convulsed with laughter."

Before he was converted he preached mere morality, but after he was called by the Holy Spirit he was zealous for the doctrines of sovereign grace, and preached the gospel in the clearest possible manner. In his ministry he was diligence itself, journeying through the counties of Cambridge, Bedford, Hertford, and Huntingdon continually, preaching upon an average from ten to twelve sermons a week, and riding from place to place on horseback. He wrote to a friend—"I fear my weekly circuits would not suit a London or a Bath divine, nor any tender evangelist that is environed with prunello. Long rides and miry roads in sharp weather.' Cold houses to sit in, with very moderate fuel, and three or four children roaring or rocking about you! Coarse food and meager liquor; lumpy beds to lie on and too short for the feet; and stiff blankets like boards for a covering. Rise at five in the morning to preach; at seven breakfast on tea that smells very sickly; at eight mount a horse, with boots never cleaned, and then ride home, praising God for all mercies."

A complaint was lodged against him, and the bishop sent for him and reproved him for preaching "at all hours and on all days." "My lord," said he, modestly, "I preach only at two seasons." "Which are they, Mr. Berridge?" "In season and out of season, my lord."

The revival which resulted from his efforts was remarkable for depth and continuance, and for the personal persecution which it brought upon the good man. The clergy and gentry made common cause with the lowest mob against him. *"The old devil"* was the only name by which he was distinguished for between twenty and thirty years,: but none of these things moved him. Crowds waited upon him wherever he journeyed, and his own church was crammed, we had almost said up to the ceiling, for we have heard of men clambering up and sitting upon the cross-beams of the roof, while the windows were filled within and without, and even the outside of the pulpit, to the very top, so that Mr. Berridge seemed almost stifled. There is no wonder that the people thronged him, for his style was so intensely earnest, homely, and simple, that every ploughman was glad to hear the gospel preached in a tongue which he could understand, and with an earnestness which he could not resist.

His discourses were not after a set fashion, and were frequently well nigh impromptu. Mr. Berridge says that sometimes on entering the pulpit he found himself unable to exercise his thoughts on his subject, and felt himself to be "like a barber's block with a wig on"; but his hearers did not think so, for they were excited to a passionate fervor by his words. On one occasion, while mounting the stairs of the pulpit at Tottenham Court Road, his memory seemed to fail him, and he commenced his sermon by saying, "I set out to this place to-night with a sack well filled with well-baked wheaten bread, which I hoped to set before you, but the bottom came out of the sack as I walked up-stairs, and I have nothing left for you but five barley loaves and a few small fishes. You will have those loaves hot from the oven; may they be food convenient for your souls."

His voice was loud, but perfectly under command; ten or fifteen thousand persons frequently composed his congregation in the open air, and he was well heard by all. People came to hear him from a distance of twenty miles, and were at Everton by seven o'clock in the morning, having set out from home soon after midnight. In the early years of his ministry he was the witness of strange scenes, when the revival took the same form as it did a few years ago in certain parts of the north of Ireland, and was accompanied by physical manifestations. The phenomena then presented were very remarkable, but we must confess that we have no faith in their *spiritual* character, and are sorry to hear of their occurrence. After a while the shoutings and contortions came to an end, and the work proceeded steadily and after the usual fashion. Amid all the excitement Berridge never lost his head or became a fanatic, neither was he exalted above measure, but remained one of the humblest and most genuine of men.

There is no doubt that his style was very remarkable, and entirely his own. In one of his letters he writes:—"I have been recruiting for Mr. Venn at Godman-chester, a very populous and wicked town near Huntingdon, and met with a patient hearing from a numerous audience. I hope he also will consecrate a few barns, and preach in them to fill up his fold at Yelling; and sure there is a cause when souls are perishing for lack of knowledge. Must salvation give place to a fanciful decency, and sinners go flocking to hell through our dread of irregularity? While irregularity in its worst shape traverses the kingdom with impunity, should not irregularity in its best shape pass without censure? I told my brother he need not fear being slandered for sheep-stealing while he only whistles the sheep to a better pasture, and meddles neither with the flesh nor the fleece, and I am sure he cannot sink much lower in credit, for he has lost his character right honestly by preaching the gospel without mincing it. The scoffing world makes no other distinction between us than between Satan and Beelzebub; we have both got tufted horns and cloven feet, only I am thought the more impudent devil of the two."

Little cared Berridge if the wicked world treated him as it did his Master, he only longed to save those who loved to revile him. His works are published in an accessible form, and all that we know of his life will be found in the memoir which precedes them; there is therefore no reason for us further to enlarge.

8
Rowland Hill, 1744—1833

IT IS NOT OUR design to write a life of Rowland Hill, but merely to sketch an outline portrait from the "eccentric" point of view. As a preacher Mr. Hill was the child of John Berridge, whose church he attended while he was a student at Cambridge, riding over to Everton every Sabbath to hear him. From that veteran he no doubt learned that freedom and simplicity of language which always distinguished him. He also associated much with John Stittle, one of Berridge's converts, and a man of very marked individuality, who preached in Green Street, Cambridge for many years. Their intimacy may be gathered from the incident recorded by William Jones:—"On one occasion, when Mr. Hill was on his way to Duxford, to preach for the Missionary Society, he suddenly exclaimed, 'I must go to Cambridge, and see the widow of an old clergyman, who lives there, for I have a message to leave with her.' He was urged not to go, but he was firm to his purpose. He spent a short time with the venerable widow, and reached Duxford just before evening service. On entering his friend Mr. Payne's house he said,' Dear me, I quite forgot to leave the message with the widow,' and seemed almost determined to return to Cambridge. He, however, remained during the service, and on being asked whether the message he had forgotten was important he replied, 'Yes, sir, I wanted the old lady, who will soon be in heaven, to give my love to Johnny Stittle, and tell him I shall soon see him again.'"

Mr. Hill's first preachings were of an itinerant character. He was glad of a church, and equally delighted with a meeting-house; but the village green, a barn, an assembly room, or a hovel were all used as they were offered. He was not reared in the lap of luxury as a preacher, nor was he surrounded by the society of unmingled aristocracy, so as to be guarded from every whiff of the air of common life. He mingled so thoroughly with the people that he became the people's man, and for ever remained so. With all the highmindedness which ought to go with nobility he mingled an unaffected simplicity and benevolence of spirit, which made him dear to persons of all ranks. He was thoroughly a man, thinking and acting for himself with all the freedom of a great emancipated mind, which bowed only at the feet of Jesus; but he was essentially a child-man, a Nathanael in whom was no guile—artless, natural, transparent, in all things unaffected, and true. He once said of a man who knew the gospel but seemed afraid to preach it, "He preaches the truth as a donkey munches a thistle—*very cautiously.*" this was exactly the opposite of his own way of doing it.

His fixed places of ministry were Surrey Chapel, and Wotton-under-Edge. He facetiously styled himself "Rector of Surrey Chapel, Vicar of Wotton, and Curate of all the fields and lanes throughout England and Wales." Surrey Chapel was called by many "The Round-house," and it was reported that its form was chosen by Mr. Hill that the devil might not have a corner to hide in. The locality is described by Berridge "as one of the worst spots in London, the very paradise of devils." It was hard by the assembling ground of Lord George.Gordon's Protestant rowdies, and was in many respects an unsavory spot, and therefore so much the more in need of the gospel The spacious structure was the center of philanthropic, educational, and religious work of all kinds, and it would be difficult to find a building from which more beneficial influences have emanated.

At Wotton, Mr. Hill lived in what he called "a paradisiacal spot," having his house near the chapel, and lovely scenery all around. He says of the village, "This place, when I first knew Gloucestershire, was filled with brutal persecutors; since they have been favored with the gospel they have been wonderfully softened." We visited the place with great interest, and were taken to the spot where dear old Rowland would sit with his telescope and watch the people coming down the neighboring hills to the meeting, and would afterwards astonish them by mentioning what he had seen. Both in London and in the country he was the universal benefactor, and mixed with all sorts of people. In London he might be teen in the streets with his hands behind him, gazing into the shop windows, and in the country the cottages and the cornfields were his study. A friend told me an anecdote which I have not met with in print. When at Wotton he heard of a woman who was noted for her sausages, and therefore called in upon her, and bought a supply. "Now, my good woman," said he, "how is it that you make such good sausages?" "Why, sir," said she, "I think it is a gift from the Almighty." Mr. Hill shook his head at this, and began to repent of his bargain, as well he might, for the articles turned out to be stale. He told the story afterwards as an instance of how people try to pass off their bad goods by canting talk, and as a proof of the fact that fanaticism is often in alliance with knavery, "A gift from the Almighty!" said he, "and yet the produce of this precious gift is good for nothing." We give this as an instance of the manner in which he turned every little incident to good account.

Our friend Mr. Charlesworth, of the Stockwell Orphanage, has written a life of Rowland Hill, which in our judgment surpasses its predecessors in giving a full length portrait of the good man, and as this is readily to be had, we refer our readers to it. We remember reading an article in one of the reviews of the day in which Mr. Hill is abused after the manner of "the Saturday." It did us great good to see how those who were before us endured the tongue of malice and survived its venom. It is clear from many remarks made by contemporary writers, and especially from the way in which one of his biographers has tried to take the very soul out of him by toning down his wit, that he was regarded by many serious people as a good brother whose infirmity was to be endured, but to be quietly censured. Now, we are not at all of this mind. Mr. Hill may have allowed his humor too much liberty, perhaps he did, but this was better than smothering it and all his other faculties, as many do, beneath a huge feather-bed of stupid formalism. When we hear our long-visaged brethren condemning all mirth, we remember the story of holy Dr. Durham, the Scotch divine, who wrote a commentary upon Solomon's Song, and another upon the Revelation. His biographers say of him that he was so grave at all times that he very seldom smiled, much less laughed, at anything. We wonder if he had any children? What kind of father must he have been? But here is the story in the old-fashioned language in which we find it. The Rev. Mr. William Guthrie, minister at Finwick, met with Mr. Durham at a gentleman's house near Glasgow, some time before his last sickness, and observing him somewhat dull, endeavored to force him to smile and laugh, by his facetious and pleasant conversation. Mr. Durham was somewhat disgusted at this innocent freedom of Mr. Guthrie, and displeased with himself that he was so merry. When Mr. Guthrie, according to the laudable custom of that family, and at their desire, prayed, he showed the greatest seriousness, composure, and devout liveliness. When he rose from prayer, Mr. Durham tenderly embraced his friend, and said to him, "O William, you are a happy man; if I had been so merry as you were before you went to pray, I should not have been serious, or in a frame for prayer, or any other religious exercises for two days." This occurrence led Mr. Durham to judge more leniently of his lively brethren, and our trust is that it may have the like effect upon any sour person who may chance to read this little book.

Mr. Hill's name is very sweet in South London, and if you chance to meet with one of his old hearers, it will do your heart goo(t to see how his eyes will sparkle at the bare mention of his name. He made religion a delight and the worship of God a pleasure; yea, he made the very memory of it to be a joy for ever to the hearts of the aged as they recall the days of their youth when Rowland Hill—dear old Rowland Hill as they like to call him—was in his glory.

9
Matthew Wilks, 1746—1829

WHAT ROWLAND HILL WAS on one side of the Thames Matthew Wilks was upon the other. He came to London in 1775, and John Berridge took part in his ordination over the Tabernacle churches which had been gathered by Whitefield. He was a person of commanding appearance, of great shrewdness, and special singularity, and, like other worthy men, he has been much belied because a vein of humor was manifest in him. This matters little, since the good man led multitudes to Jesus, and was a faithful pastor to the flock which he gathered. He was one of the fathers of the London Missionary Society, the Evangelical Magazine, the Irish Evangelical Society, the Bible Society, and the Religious Tract Society in fact, from his great practical wisdom, he was called upon to be a leader in all kinds of Christian work.

Many an odd thing has fallen from his lips; as for instance when he wished to explain the text, "See that ye walk circumspectly," he pictured a cat walking upon the top of a high wall covered with bits of glass bottles. We have heard this illustration quoted with ridicule, but we fail to see any objection to it. Let anyone watch a cat in such circumstances, and then find a better instance of circumspect walking if he can. We do not believe the tradition that he rebuked the head-dresses of the day by preaching upon "top (k)not come down," which is a cutting from the text, "Let him that is upon the house top not come down": but we have met a gentleman who said that he saw him hold up a small pair of scales when preaching from "Thou art weighed in the balances." We do not wish to doubt our informant, but we think it probable that no actual scales were present, but that Wilks so imitated the holding up of balances and the act of weighing that in after years the memory became a little aided by the imagination, and actual scales and weights were supplied in the narrator's mind.

Mr. Wilks' anniversary sermon for the London Missionary Society was a very striking one. Certainly the text was remarkable enough. "The children gather wood, and the fathers kindle the fire, and the women knead their dough, to make cakes to the queen of heaven, and to pour out drink offerings unto other gods, that they may provoke me to anger:" Jeremiah 7:18. "When the text was announced, in the midst of a crowded assembly, every eye seemed to express astonishment at the preacher's choice. He had not proceeded far, however, in his undertaking, when the feeling of astonishment gave place to pure delight, when all seemed convinced that though the text was uncommon, it was by no means inappropriate. Having glanced at the idolatrous worship of the queen of heaven, the ardor of the worshippers, and the persons employed in it; he then said, 'I will *contrast* your objects, *compare* your ardor, and *muster* your agents.' The appeal was admirably directed, and energetically sustained, and from the hearing and perusal of that part of it which referred to the agents, viz., *the men, women, and children,* arose the system of auxiliary institutions which now pervades the whole country, and combines in its support young and old, rich and poor; such an extraordinary effect has seldom, perhaps, sprung from the preaching of a single discourse. Irrespective, however, of its impression as delivered from the pulpit, it possesses considerable merit, as an argument and as a composition."

Beyond a wretched little memoir and a few mere outlines of sermons, nothing remains of all the great and good things which were spoken by Mr. Wilks, and the stories told of him relate to him rather as a man than as a preacher. My venerable friend Mr. George Rogers has given me the following note:—

"Matthew Wilks was very comic in his appearance, in his voice, and in his language. Like Mr. Hill, he was sound in is gospel views, was very useful, and deservedly popular. He has called upon me, and frequently engaged me to preach for him at 'both Tabs.,' as he called them. He had a stern aspect, but a tender heart. Two incidents I may mention, which I received from a mutual friend of myself and Mr. Wilks, and which I believe to be authentic. When John Williams was recommended to the London Missionary Society, and nearly all the directors were opposed to him, he found a determined supporter in Mr. Wilks, who even went so far in pressing the point as to be charged with being overbearing. When the debate was over, Mr. Wilks went into the room where Mr. Williams was waiting for the decision of the committee and said, 'Well, young man, you have been accepted, but if it, had not been for my overbearing disposition you never would have got in.' This was Williams the martyr at Erromanga.

"A minister from the West of England having called upon Mr. Wilks, and informed him that he was in great distress of mind on account of debt; Mr. Wilks said, 'You are a great fool; you ought not to get in debt.' 'Oh,' he replied, 'it gradually accumulated, and I could not help it. My wife was ill, and some of my children died, and my income is very small.' 'How much do you owe?' 'About £70? 'Then you are a great fool. I want you to preach at Greenwich next Sunday.' 'Oh, I am too much dejected.' 'But I say you must go, and I will send a note to the gentleman with whom you must dine.' Returning to Mr. Wilks on Monday morning, he told him the gentleman with whom he dined gave him £10. 'Well,' said Mr. Wilks, 'but you are a fool for getting into debt for all that.' He then produced another £10, and said he had obtained that from another gentleman for him. Observing him to be much affected by this, Mr. Wilks added,' Still you are a great fool.' He then produced another £10, called him a fool more vehemently than before, and thus continued to put £10 before him again and again and to scold him until the whole £70 was produced; and then he said, 'Now go home, and don't be such a fool as to get into debt again.' This showed a great knowledge of human nature, for he thus kept the good man from being overwhelmed by the great and unexpected relief."

But Mr. Wilks could be fearfully severe, and when he had doubts about the ability or character of a candidate for the ministry he showed no mercy. On one occasion he had badgered and brow-beaten a young man to such a degree that he was scarcely able to answer a single question. "Man," said Mr. Wilks, "you'll never be fit for the ministry: you seem to know nothing at all: can you tell the difference between me and Moses?" "Hoot, toot, Mr. Wilks," interposed good Dr. Waugh, anxious to release the young victim, "you should na' put such a question as that to the lad; but if you like I'll tell you the difference between Moses and you: *Moses was the meekest of men.*"

More genial was his mode of finding a wife for a brother minister. He sent him to the lady's house with this laconic note:—

"My dear madam,—Allow me to introduce to you my worthy friend, the Rev. Mr. A—

"If you're a cat,
You'll smell a rat!

"Yours truly,
"MATT. WILKS."

The lady found it needful to request the gentleman to explain the letter; this led them into pleasant conversation, and into mutual admiration, which ended in marriage. The mystery of the cat and the rat was thus solved.

We may not imitate his drollery, but it would be a happy circumstance if all ministers as diligently read the Bible as he did, for he read it through carefully four times in the year. He was careful that his co-pastors and assistants were well remunerated, but he would only receive £200 a year himself, and of that he gave £100 away. He loved the poor, and his poor people loved him. His power over his members was very great, for it was founded in love. The common people heard him gladly, and among them he enjoyed a long and fruitful ministry. The works which he commenced have been perpetuated, especially the societies which he helped to inaugurate. The Lord has thus enabled his work to endure the fiery ordeal of time, which is a severe test, causing many pretentious ministries to pass away as smoke. Call him eccentric if you please, but our prayer shall be to the Lord that we may share in the blessing which rests on the labors of Matthew Wilks. "Establish thou the work of our hands upon us; yea, the work of our hands establish thou it."

10
William Dawson, 1773—1841

MR. WILLIAM DAWSON, THE Yorkshire farmer and Methodist preacher, should be mentioned among the eccentrics, but not on account of any great use of wit in his preaching. Gross falsehoods were forged concerning him, and he was made to appear as a mere comic actor by the ribald world, but there was nothing about his preaching to deserve it. He was apt at repartee, and there was a slight mixture of drollery in his sermons, but he was mainly distinguished for his wonderful dramatic power, by which he made everything stand out before the people's eyes, and thus created the deepest impressions. In a note from Dr. Osborn to us, that gentleman says: "Wit was not Dawson's specialty, it was the intense activity and fervor of his imagination, with a basis of sound doctrine and sound character, which was the source of his power, and a mighty power it was." In a brief sketch of Mr. Dawson, by Mr. R. A. West, we read the following description of his outer man, which lets us see the farmer and the preacher combined:—

"I first heard Mr. Dawson from the pulpit in the year 1828. His apparel and demeanor struck me as unclerical. True, he wore a black coat and vest, and a white neck-cloth, but his lower extremities were encased in a pair of drab breeches, and he wore what are technically called 'top boots,' such as are, and were at the time, universally worn in England by substantial farmers as a part of their Sunday or market-day attire. He crossed the floor of the chapel on his way to the pulpit with a rolling gait, as though he were traversing a ploughed field, with a hand in each pocket of his drabs, half whistling, half humming the air of a good old Methodist tune. Of this he was apparently unconscious, for his eyes were turned downward in a reverie, and he seemed shut in from all surrounding objects. In all my subsequent knowledge of him I never saw a repetition of the mood."

He was always natural and farmer-like; the smell as of a field that the Lord had blessed was upon him, and the multitude delighted to hear him. His power in setting an illustration before his hearers will be seen from the following: "Preaching on the returning prodigal, Mr. Dawson paused, looked at the door, and shouted out, after he had depicted him in his wretchedness,' Yonder he comes, slipshod! Make way—make way— make way, there.' Such was the approach to reality, that a considerable part of the congregation turned to the door, some rising on their feet, under the momentary impression that some one was entering the chapel in the state described. In the same sermon, paraphrasing the father's replying to the son that was angry, and would not go in, he said: 'Be not offended; surely a *calf* may do for a *prodigal,* shoes for a *prodigal,* a *ring* and a *robe* for a *prodigal,* but ALL I have is THINE,.' As to the more striking effect, when pointing to the door, similar results were produced when referring to the Witch of Endor. His picturing took such hold on the imagination, that on exclaiming,' Stand by—stand by! There she is!' some of the poor people inadvertently directed their eyes downward, where his own eye was fixed, and the spot to which he was pointing, as if she were about to rise from beneath their feet, and become visible to the congregation."

The next extract is part of a peroration of a sermon from Revelation 6:7, 8, "And when he had opened the fourth seal, I heard the voice of the fourth beast say, Come and see," etc. "'Come and see,' then, the awful condition of an unsaved sinner. Open your eyes, sinner, and see it yourself. *There* he is in the broad road of ruin; every step he takes is deeper in sin; every breath he draws feeds his corruption; every moment takes him farther from heaven and nearer hell. Onward, onward he is going—death and hell are after him quickly, untiringly they pursue him—with swift but noiseless hoof the pale horse and his pale rider are tracking the godless wretch. See! see! they are getting nearer, they are overtaking him." At this moment the stillness of the congregation was so complete that the ticking of the clock could be distinctly heard in every part of the chapel. Upon this, with a facility peculiarly his own, he promptly seized, and without seeming interruption. Leaning over the pulpit in the attitude of attention, and fixing his keen eye upon those who sat immediately before him, he continued in an almost supernatural whisper, "Hark! hark! that swift rider is coming, and judgment is following him. That is his untiring footstep! Hark!"— and then imitating for a moment or two the beat of the pendulum, he exclaimed in the highest pitch of his voice, "Lord, save the sinner! save him! Death is upon him, and hell follows! See, the long arm is raised! The final dart is poised! O my God, save him—save him—for if the rider overtakes that poor sinner, unpardoned and unsaved, and strikes his blow, down he falls, and backward he drops—hell behind him, and as he falls backward, he looks upward, and shrieks—'Lost! lost! lost! Time lost; Sabbaths lost; means lost; soul lost; heaven lost! ALL LOST, and lost for ever!' Backward he drops; all his sins seem to hang round his neck like so many millstones as he plunges into the burning abyss. 'Come and see.' Lord, save him! O my God, save him! 'Come and see.' Blessed be God! The rider has not overtaken him yet; there is time and space yet for that poor sinner: he may be saved yet—he has not dropped into hell. 'Come and see.' The horse and the rider have not overtaken you yet; there is, therefore, an 'accepted time,' there is a 'day of salvation'! 'Come and see.' There is God the Father inviting you; God the Father commanding you; God the Father swearing he has no pleasure in your death, but in your life. There is Jesus Christ come to seek you. He has Cravelied thirty years to save you. He is dying on the cross. With his outstretched arms he says, 'Come unto me, and I will give you rest.' 'He that believeth in me shall never die!'" The effect was so overwhelming that two of the congregation fainted, and it required all the preacher's tact and self-command to ride through the storm, which his own vivid imagination had aroused.

Those must have been stirring services in which his hearers audibly responded to his appeals. On one occasion when he exhorted his hearers to give their hearts to the Lord, he added, with his hand on his breast and his eyes towards heaven, "Here's mine." A voice from the gallery called out, "Here's mine, too, Billy!"

Preaching at Ancoats, Manchester, on Judges 8:4,—"Faint, yet pursuing," every eye seemed at one time suffused with tears; and when people and preacher were craned up to the highest pitch of feeling, a momentary pause ensued, during which the clock struck *twelve,* and broke the stillness that reigned, like the hammer on the bell at a watch night, on the departure of the old year. In an instant he darted his eyes to the front of the gallery, and personifying the timepiece, said—"You may speak, clock, but I am not done yet." Though no apparent expectation existed on the part of the auditory that he would close his discourse with the hour, yet it had all the effect of reviving disappointed hope, and threw a gleam of sunshine into every countenance.

William Dawson was a man by himself. When nature formed him she broke the mould, but we could have wished that she had given us at least another after his manner and order. Of his power in witty answers we will only give one specimen, and then close our notice. The following dialogue was held between Dawson and a fault-finding gentleman.

Gentleman. "I had the pleasure of hearing you yesterday."

Mr. Dawson. "I hope you not only heard but profited."

Gent. "Yes, I did; but I don't like those prayer-meetings at the close. They destroy all the good previously received."

Mr. D. "You should have united with the people in them."

Gent. "I went into the gallery, where I hung over the front, and saw the whole, but I could get no good; I lost, indeed, all the benefit I had received during the sermon."

Mr. D. "It is easy to account for that,"

Gent. "How so?"

Mr. D. "You mounted the top of the house; and on looking down your neighbor's chimney to see what kind of a *fire* he kept, you got your eyes filled with smoke. Had you entered by the door, and gone into the room, and mingled with the family around the household hearth, *you* would have enjoyed the benefit of the fire as well as they. Sir, you have got the smoke in your eyes."

11
Jacob Gruber, 1778—1850

WHEN THE POPULATION OF the United States was sparse and widely scattered, the public services of religion could not have been maintained at all if the Lord had not raised up a race of zealous itinerants, who passed rapidly from one hamlet or homestead to another, and by their intense earnestness kept alive the sacred fire. We allude to a period ranging from one hundred years back to within half-a-century of the present date. The men of that time were necessarily strong physically, or they could not have borne the hardships of their wandering mission, and they were also sturdy mentally, and needed to be so, for they met with people who required vigorous handling. Of course they were rough and unrefined—what could they have effected had they been other-wine? Of what use would a razor be in clearing a forest? Very frequently they were wildly humorous as well as vehemently zealous; but probably this play of their spirits was needful to keep them from sinking down under the burdens of their uncomfortable and trying circumstances. At any rate, they did the work which God gave them to do, and left America a Christian instead of a heathen country, which last it might readily have become had it not been for their efforts. We do not commend all that they did, much less hold them up for imitation; but we think it profitable to see how others did their work, and therefore we would describe Jacob Gruber, of whom his contemporaries said, "He is a character, and copies no man." We shall do little more than give extracts from a biography written by W. P. Strickland, which has not been published in this country. We shall make a long chapter of this, because we shall regard Gruber as a sort of spacimen American evangelist of the backwoods' order.

"At the beginning of the present century there appeared at the seat of the Philadelphia Conference a young man who was impressed with the conviction that it was his duty to preach. His parents were of German descent, and had been brought up in the faith of the great leader of the Reformation. The German Reformed Church for many years had the exclusive control of the religious interests of the neighborhood. The time, however, came when this quiet was broken. Two itinerant Methodist preachers had divided up the country into circuits, and, claiming to be successors of the apostles, thought it no robbery to imitate them in traversing the country, and preaching the gospel wherever they found an open door. The strangeness of their manner, and the wonderful earnestness of their preaching, attracted the attention of the people, particularly the younger portion, and the cabins and barns where they held forth were crowded.

"Young Gruber listened to these circuit preachers with amazement; and though they were denounced by the staid and sober Reformers as wild and fanatical, he nevertheless felt strangely drawn to their meetings. There was such a fervor in their prayers, such a zeal and earnestness in their preaching, and such a power in their songs, that he was entirely fascinated, and soon became convinced of the need of conversion. His prayers for a change of heart were soon answered, and with gladness he went with his parents to the place of meeting, and with them joined the Methodist church.

"That the reader may have a correct description of the religious condition of this particular neighborhood, we give an account prepared by Gruber himself. He says: 'The Methodist preachers came into the neighborhood, and held several meetings. As the result of their labors a revival commenced, and quite a number of persons were converted, and professed a knowledge of sins forgiven.' Some of the members of the German minister's church went to the old gentleman, expressing a desire to know something about this new doctrine. In reply to their inquiries about the knowledge of forgiveness, he said: 'I have been a preacher more than twenty years, and I do not know my sins forgiven, and indeed it is impossible that anyone should know it.' It was not considered very wonderful by some that this preacher should be in darkness on that subject, as he frequently became intoxicated. An aged woman, a member of the German church, at one of the revival meetings where some were praising God for having pardoned their sins, stood thoughtfully shaking her head and said, 'It could not be, for if they had to answer a hundred and sixty questions, as she had before she got religion, they would learn that it could not be obtained in such quick time.'

"Among the early itinerants who visited Pennsylvania about this time was the eccentric Valentine Cook. He was fresh from the halls of Cokesbury College, and perhaps the first native college-bred preacher that had appeared in the American Methodist church. When Cook made his appearance, and it was rumored that he was a graduate of a college, he attracted general attention. The German Reformed, like several other churches we could name, entertained the idea that no man could possibly be qualified to preach who had not received a classical education; and hence vastly more respect was paid to Cook than to any of his colleagues in the ministry. His learning, however, did not always avail to insure him respect, as the following incident will show:—After travelling a whole day without refreshment in a region where he was not known, he halted in the evening at the house of a German, and asked if he could obtain feed for his horse and something for himself to eat. Being a tall, rough-looking specimen of humanity, the good woman, who was engaged in spinning, took him to be an Irishman. She was not at all favorably impressed with his appearance, but at her husband's request she procured a lunch for him and returned to her wheel, saying to her husband somewhat petulantly in German, she hoped the Irishman would choke in eating. After Cook had finished his repast he asked the privilege to pray, which being granted he knelt down and offered up a fervent petition in German. In his prayer he besought the Lord to bless the kind woman at the wheel and give her a new heart, that she might be better disposed towards strangers. Such a personal reflection was more than the good woman could stand, and she left her wheel and ran from the house overwhelmed with chagrin at her wicked wish.

"We mention these incidents for the propose of giving the reader some idea of the times in which young Gruber commenced his religious career. Being a sprightly lad, he was soon called out to exercise his gifts in public prayer and exhortation. As usual in such cases, a storm of persecution arose, not only from those who were outside the church and the family, but from his own household. Father, mother, brothers, and sisters, as if by one consent, rose up against the young exhorter, and he was obliged to leave home and seek more congenial quarters elsewhere. Some of the more zealous Methodists interpreted this differently from what young Jacob had imagined, and persuaded him that it was a clear indication of Providence that it was his duty to abandon everything for the exclusive work of the ministry. This interpretation of Providence was soon after verified. As he went on his way afoot and alone to the town of Lancaster he met one of the itinerants, who in a short conversation convinced him of the duty of entering upon the ministry, and sent him to an adjoining circuit to fill a vacancy. He accordingly procured a horse and went to the appointment.

"As the conference embraced sickly regions in its territory, he knew not but he might be sent by the intrepid Bishop Asbury to some one of these localities, if for no other propose than to try his mettle. Many a young man has finished his course in one year's service; but it was not to be so with Gruber. He had a powerful constitution, an iron frame capable of enduring an amount of hardship, labor, and fatigue which made him the wonder of all his ministerial companions.

"The second year of our young itinerant's ministry was spent where vast tracts of wilderness interposed between the appointments, and new hardships were to be endured. Nothing daunted, he scaled the mountains, penetrated the woods, and sought the cabins nestling among them, that he might preach the gospel to their inmates. Here he labored with the most unremitting zeal and diligence. Through his fervent appeals many were awakened and converted.

"At a certain place on this circuit there lived a man who had been in great distress of mind, bordering on despair. He wept much and prayed almost constantly, but found no relief. He was visited by Gruber, who conversed with him for a considerable length of time, quoting such passages of the Bible as were applicable to his case. He could not, however, be persuaded that any promise was for him, as he believed his day of mercy and hope was gone for ever. The following colloquy then ensued between Gruber and the despairing man:

"'What will become of you?' 'I shall be lost.' 'Where will you go?' 'To hell.' 'But if you go there you will have it all to yourself.' 'What do you mean?' 'I mean just what I say: if you go to hell weeping and praying, you will scare all the devils away, for I never heard or read of one going to hell weeping and praying.' At this a smile came over his face like sunshine on a cloud; his despair was gone, and hope full and joyous sprang up in his soul.

"At the next conference Gruber was sent to the Winchester circuit, having for a colleague a young man by the name of Richards. This young itinerant in a great measure destroyed his usefulness by getting the crotchet into his head that, to maintain ministerial dignity, he must put on extra airs of reserve and sanctity. A 'sad countenance,' as our old English version has it, in the description of the Pharisees in the days of the Savior, is not a true index of spirituality. One of the old preachers who had outlived his day, and was constantly harping upon one string—'Ye are fallen! ye are fallen!' remarked on a certain occasion that he wished some of the old preachers were as solemn as that young man. Bishop Asbury, who was present when this remark was made, smilingly said: 'Do you make any allowance for solids and fluids?' We recollect a reply once made by a lighthearted, joyous, talented young preacher to a pious lady, who reprovingly said to him,' I wish you would be as serious as Brother C.' 'Ah!' said the young brother, laughingly, 'when I get the dyspepsia as bad as he has it, I will, no doubt, be equally serious.'

"He had now been six years in the work of the ministry, and had exhibited such good proof of his fidelity and success that the good Bishop Asbury deemed him qualified for the more responsible post of presiding elder, and accordingly, in the year 1807, he was appointed to the presidency of Greenbrier district. It embraced a wild region of country in Virginia, said to be the roughest in the bounds of the Baltimore Conference. To use his own language, he had 'hard work, rough fare, and bad roads;' but by way of offset to these disadvantages he had 'great meetings.' Towards the close of the year camp-meetings were held on every circuit, and hundreds were converted. Indeed, a camp-meeting in those days without numerous conversions and large accessions to the church would have been a great wonder.

"At that time even a quarterly meeting was considered dull and profitless unless souls were converted and added to the church, and a revival inaugurated for the coming quarter. In describing these camp-meetings, Gruber said: 'Some complained about too much wildfire, and called the preachers the fire company; but we wanted fire that would warm and melt, not tame-fire, fox-fire, and the like." During the three years on this district he experienced many hardships. In describing his labors he says: 'One very cold night in the winter I took a path for a near way to my stopping-place, but got out of my course, wandered about among the hills and mountains, and went to the top of one of them to see clearings, or hear dogs bark, or roosters crow, but all in vain. After midnight the moon arose; I could then see my track. The snow was knee-deep, and I went back till I got into the right course, and reached my lodgings between four and five o'clock in the morning. The family was alarmed, and said I was late, but I called it early. After lying down and sleeping a little I arose, and getting breakfast departed on my day's journey, filling two appointments.'

"At the end of his first year on the district he had a line of appointments reaching to Baltimore. On his route he passed through a wild, mountainous region, traversed by a dim path. Not a single cabin was to be found in a distance of twenty miles. He struck for the path on the mountain about ten o'clock, but, had not proceeded many miles before he found it covered up knee-deep in snow, and not a single track to be seen. He picked his way, however, as best he could, and traveled on. During the day it began to rain, which rendered his journey still more uncomfortable. At length he reached Cheat River, and found it considerably swollen, with ice in the middle. When he reached the ice it was with difficulty he dismounted, and then making his horse leap upon it he again mounted. The ice did not break, and he was enabled to reach the other shore. He traveled on in the woods until night overlook him, when he lost his path and became entangled in the forest. The rain, which had been pouring down, now changed into snow, and the wind blew furiously. Besides all this, it was becoming increasingly cold. What to do he knew not, except to pray. The night was spent sitting on his horse. Above the roar of the storm he could hear the scream of the panther and the howl of the wolf. It was a dreadful night; but morning came, and with it he found the path, and in a short time found himself at the house of a friend. The family were alarmed at seeing him, and expressed their surprise at his undertaking so perilous a journey, as no person had been known to pass through that portion of the wilderness before in winter. Neither himself nor horse had tasted a morsel of food since they started, but riley were both inured to hardships, and suffered but little in consequence. After obtaining some refreshment, he started to his appointment, thankful for his escape from the dangers through which he had passed.

"Gruber gives several incidents that occurred at camp-meetings. 'In one camp,' he says, 'some bold sinners came to fight for their master, the devil; but our captain, Immanuel, made prisoners of them, and then made them "free indeed." One fine, strong, good-looking young man among the mourners was in great distress, and found no relief until he drew a large pistol out of his pocket, with which he intended to defend himself if any one should offer to speak to him on the subject of religion. When he laid it on the bench beside him the Lord blessed him, and gave him a great victory over his foes.'"

Gruber was dreadfully severe upon all worldliness, and especially upon foppishness in dress, which he denounced and ridiculed. A little of his healthy banter might be useful in these dressy days.

"While preaching in a certain place on one occasion an unusually tall lady entered. On seeing her he stopped preaching and said: 'Make room for that lady; one might have thought she was tall enough to be seen without the plumage of that pird in her ponnet.' Some days afterward the lady met Gruber and complained that he had treated her rudely. 'O sister,' he replied, 'was that you? Well, I did not know it was you; I thought *you* had more sense.'

"At a camp-meeting on a certain occasion, where considerable difficulty was experienced in getting the people to observe order, from the number of young persons who were walking about, collecting in groups, and engaged in conversation, the presiding eider, in the most respectful and courteous terms, requested them to be seated. Not seeming to understand, or not caring to comply with the request, the young people paid no attention whatever to what was said, but kept up their walking and talking. Gruber, who was present, felt greatly aggrieved, and rising in the stand he roared out, 'Mr. Presiding Elder, you called those young folks gentlemen and ladies, and they did not know what you meant!' He then added, 'Boys, come right along and take seats here,' pointing to the right; 'and you, gals, come up and take your seats here on the left.' Earnest and peremptory as he was, yet so comical was his manner that their attention was at once arrested, and they came smilingly forward and took their seats."

To us this mode of address would have seemed rude and irritating, and very unlikely to secure the desired end, but Jacob knew the people he had to deal with, and how to handle them. To some persons a polite address sounds like affectation, and, taking it to mean nothing, they let it go in at one ear and out at the other; a plain, blunt, commanding mode of speech they see to be earnestly intended, and yield to it. Very much depends upon the character of the persons to whom we speak, and something also upon our own age and position: it would never do for a young minister fresh from college to address those of his own age as girls and boys, neither would such a style of admonition be acceptable to our educated young people even if the oldest divine so accosted them. The practical lesson is to have the thing done somehow, if it is right, and to use just such a method of speaking as will be best calculated to secure it. The dread of sinning against etiquette is as much to be avoided as the vulgarity which causes needless offense. The case in which Gruber acted so oddly will perhaps never occur to us, and, if it does, we must use our best judgment, and hope to succeed as he did.

"At a camp-meeting near Baltimore, after the trumpet had been blown announcing the time for closing the exercises in the praying circles, one of them, unwilling to stop, kept on singing and praying. Gruber, somewhat impatient, shouted out at the top of his voice, 'That's right, brothers, blow all the fire out.'" Often has the same thought occurred to our mind when we have seen unwise brethren ranting on long after the "spirit of supplication" has been fully exhausted. Long prayers and long addresses blow out the fire which they are intended to increase.

Gruber's later years were more calm and quiet, but they were not quite devoid of stirring incident. The sinners of his day were as eccentric as the preachers who sought to win them. If they were assailed from the pulpit with rough weapons, they knew how to be vigorously offensive in return. Gruber says—

"I was sent a second year to Dauphin circuit. Nothing extraordinary took place, only some fellows of the baser sort made an attempt to blow up our meeting-house in Harrisburg. On a Sunday night after preaching they got in at a window, put something under the pulpit with powder in it and a match. It made a report like a cannon,, tore up the pulpit, and broke the glass out of some of the windows. We soon, however, had all repaired, and pursued our course. My colleague this year was a poor thing hunting a fortune. He found out who was rich; but the girls found out that he was lazy, so he had little success in winning souls, and none in getting a wife. Some young men think if they can only get married (the sooner the better) they will be at once in paradise; and some young women have an idea that if they can only get a preacher they will have an angel for certain; but more than one has been disappointed very much.

"While in attendance at conference in Philadelphia, in 1830, he was appointed to preach in his old charge, St. George's. He took for his text Psalm 84:4: 'Blessed are they that dwell in thy house, they will be still praising thee.' Retaining a keen sense of the unkind manner in which he was treated by some of the members of that charge, which resulted in his removal at the end of the first year, he felt disposed to let his hearers know it by witty and cutting allusions. Under the head of "The Character of those who dwell in the House of the Lord," he mentioned three characteristics,

"'1. *They were a humble people,* willing to occupy a humble place in the church; indeed, any place so that they might be permitted to abide in the church; but there were some people who were so proud and ambitious that, unless they could be like the first king of Israel, from the shoulders up higher than everybody else, they wouldn't come into the house at all, but hang about the doors.

"'2. *They were a contented people.* If everything did not exactly suit them, they made the best of it, and tried to get along as well as they could; but there are many who are so uneasy and fidgety that they can't *dwell* in the church, but are continually running in and out, disturbing themselves and everybody else.

"'3. *They were a satisfied people,* always finding something good, and thankful for it. Let who would be their preacher they could always get something that would give them instruction and encouragement. But some people are never satisfied, but are always finding fault with their preacher; some preach too loud, and some too long, and some say so many hard and queer things, and some are so prosy and dull that they can't be fed at all and are never satisfied. If the multitude that were fed by the Savior had been like these people they never would have been fed. If one had cried out, "John, you shan't feed me, Peter shall "; and another had said, "Andrew shall feed me, but James shan't "; and another, "I want all bread and no fish"; and others, "I want all fish and no bread," how could they have been fed? Such dissatisfied people cannot dwell in the house of the Lord. If they are not turned out they will soon die out: they can't live.'"

"Though he was sometimes severe in his criticisms on young preachers, he always entertained for them a fatherly affection, and sought only to correct their errors: but we cannot think he was justified in publicly rebuking a foolish stripling who had attacked Methodism, by asking the Lord, 'to make his heart as soft as his head, for then he might do good.'

"A young preacher, desirous of improving his style as a pulpit orator, and having great confidence in Father Gruber, wrote to him for advice. The young man had contracted the habit of prolonging his words, especially when under the influence of great excitement. Deeming this the most important defect in his elocution, Gruber sent him the following laconic reply:—

"'Dear Ah! Brother Ah!—When-ah you-ah go-ah to-ah preach-ah, takeah care ah you-ah don't-ah say-ah Ah-ah! Yours-ah,
"JACOB-AH GRUBER-AH.'

"But one of the oddest reproofs I ever knew him to administer was on a larger scale, and proved not less effectual. In a certain church the congregation had an unseemly practice of turning their backs on the pulpit during a certain portion of the singing. One Sabbath Mr. Gruber conducted the service, and, as usual, the whole congregation simultaneously turned round, presenting their backs to the preacher. Instantly the preacher, to be even with them, turned round also, presenting his back to the congregation. When the time for prayer came, at the close of the hymn, the congregation were astonished to find the preacher turned from them and gazing at the wall. The hint was enough; they did not repeat the objectionable practice."

Mr. Martin thus describes the closing scene of Gruber's life:—

"He was taken suddenly worse on the evening of the twenty-third of May, having several attacks of fainting or swooning. He gradually grew weaker and weaker, until forty-eight hours afterwards the scene closed. He was conscious that his end was rapidly approaching, and sighed for the happy release. He requested brother Blake, if it could be ascertained when he was about to die, to collect a few brethren and sisters around him, that they might (to use his own words) *'See me safe off;* and as I am going, all join in full chorus and sing:—"On Jordan's stormy banks I stand.'"

"A few hours before he died he asked Brother Blake whether he could stand it another night, and was answered that in his judgment he could not. 'Then,' said he, 'to-morrow I shall spend my first Sabbath in heaven! Last Sabbath in the church on earth, next Sabbath in the church above!' and with evident emotion added,—

> 'Where congregations ne'er break up,
> And Sabbaths have no end.'

"Brother Blake, perceiving that he was fast sinking, in accordance with his request, the hymn he had selected was sung; but ere it was concluded his consciousness was gone. The singing ceased, a deathlike stillness reigned, only broken by his occasional respiration. An overwhelming sense of the presence of God melted every heart. A minute more and his happy spirit winged its way to its long-sought rest. He died in the seventy-second year of his age."

If any judge too severely the personal peculiarities of such a man, we would urge them to do better; but to us it seems more than probable that were preachers more in earnest we should see more of what are called eccentricities, which are often only the ensigns of real zeal, and the tokens that a man is both natural and intense. If a fisherman can catch fish with silk lines and artificial bait, let him be thankful; but if with a superior tackle he is unsuccessful, it shows a very proud spirit if he indulges in harsh criticisms of the style and manner of brethren who succeed better than himself in the gospel.fishery. "Every man in his own order" is a good rule. Apollos may be polished and Cephas blunt, but so far as they are honest, prayerful, and true to the Gospel, God will bless them both, and it ill becomes them to pick holes in each other's coats. We would never say to a man, "Be eccentric"; but if he cannot help being' so, we would not have him otherwise. The leaning tower of Pisa owes much of its celebrity to its leaning, and although it certainly is not a safe model for architects, we would by no means advise the taking of it down. Ten to one any builder who tried to erect another would create a huge ruin, and therefore it would not be a safe precedent; but there it is, and who wishes it were other than it is? Serve the Lord, brother, with your very best, and seek to do still better, and whatever your peculiarities, the grace of God will be glorified in you.

12
Edward Taylor, 1793—1871

WE WOULD NOW INTRODUCE "Father Taylor," the Sailor Preacher of Boston. Not Father Taylor of California, who is a younger man, but Edward Taylor, of the Bethel,—the man whom Charles Dickens thus described in his "American Notes":—

"The only preacher I heard in Boston was Mr. Taylor, who addresses himself peculiarly to seamen, and who was once a mariner himself. I found his chapel down among the shipping, in one of the narrow, old, waterside streets, with a gay blue flag waving freely from its roof. The preacher looked a weather-beaten, hard-featured man, of about six or eight and fifty; with deep lines graven as it were into his face, dark hair, and a stern, keen eye. Yet the general character of his countenance was pleasant and agreeable. His text was, 'Who is this that cometh up from the wilderness, leaning upon her beloved?'

"He handled this text in all kinds of ways, and twisted it into all manner of shapes; but always ingeniously, and with a rude eloquence, well adapted to the comprehension of his hearers. Indeed, if I be not mistaken, he studied their sympathies and understandings much more than the display of his own powers. His imagery was all drawn from the sea, and from the incidents of a seaman's life; and was often remarkably good. He spoke to them of 'that glorious man, Lord Nelson,' and of Coilingwood; and drew nothing in, as the saying is, by the head and shoulders, but brought it to bear upon his purpose, naturally, and with a sharp mind to its effect. Sometimes, when much excited with his subject, he had an odd way of taking his great quarto Bible under his arm and pacing up and down the pulpit with it; looking steadily down, meantime, into the midst of the congregation. Thus, when he applied his text to the first assemblage of his hearers, and pictured the wonder of the church at their presumption in forming a congregation among themselves, he stopped short with his Bible under his arm and pursued his discourse after this manner:—

"' Who are these, who are they, who are these fellows? where do they come from? Where are they going to? Come from! What's the answer?' leaning out of the pulpit, and pointing downward with his right hand: 'From below!' starting back again, and looking at the sailors before him: 'From below, my brethren, from under the hatches of sin, battened down above you by the evil one. That's where you come from!' a walk up and down the pulpit: 'and where are you going?' stopping abruptly; 'where are you going? Aloft!' very softly, and pointing upward: '.Aloft!' louder: 'Aloft!' louder still: 'That's where you are going, with a fair wind, all taut and trim, steering direct for heaven in its glory, where there are no storms or foul weather, and where the wicked cease from troubling and the weary are at rest.' Another walk: 'That's where you're going to, my friends. That's it. That's the place. That's the port. That's the haven. It's a blessed harbor—still water there, in all changes of the winds and tides; no driving ashore upon the rocks, or slipping your cables and running out to sea, there: Peace, peace, peace, all peace!' Another walk, and putting the Bible under his left arm: 'What! these fellows are coming from the wilderness, are they? Yes. From the dreary, blighted wilderness of iniquity, whose only crop is death. But do they lean upon anything—do they lean upon nothing, these poor seamen?' Three raps upon the Bible: 'Ah, yes. Yes. They lean upon the arm of their beloved,' three more raps: 'upon the arm of their beloved,'—three more, and a walk: 'Pilot, guiding star, and compass all in one, to all hands—here it is '—three more:' Here it is. They can do their seaman's duty manfully, and be easy in their minds in the utmost peril and danger, with this'—two more: 'They can come, even these poor fellows can come, from the wilderness leaning on the arm of their beloved, and go up—up—up,' raising his hand higher and higher, at every repetition of the word, so that he stood with it at last stretched above his head, regarding them in a strange rapt manner, and pressing the book triumphantly to his breast, until he gradually subsided into some other portion of his discourse."

We are not so enamoured of Charles Dickens as to consider his verdict upon a preacher to be of any material consequence with reference to the man's real usefulness: but as a judge of vivacity of manner, and power of style, no better critic could be found.

Mr. Taylor's first regular recognized official holding-forth was before a quarterly Methodist Conference, assembled to test his qualifications. It has been reported that upon this occasion he had the coolness to select as his text the words, "By the life of Pharaoh, surely ye are spies;" but his biographer says that although those words might have been worked into the sermon, the real text was a more humble but equally singular one, "I pray thee, let me live." He adds, that the triers saw that his fervor and talents were more than an offset for his defects; and in answer to his prayer, they "let him live." We do not see how they could have done otherwise, for no Conference would have been strong enough to kill him.

After itinerating for some few years, the man and his mission met, and Father Taylor took up his abode in Boston, as a minister of the Methodist Episcopal Church, specially set apart to labor among sailors. His chapel, at first, held about five hundred hearers, and was immediately filled to its utmost capacity. He began in 1828 in full revival vigor, frequently preaching four times a day. To him it never occurred to polish his style, and prune away its power: he spoke as his heart prompted him, and worked as the Holy Spirit moved him. He did work enough for two men, and had a double blessing upon it. In a very short time Boston felt his power, and its wealth and its culture were at his feet as well as its poverty and roughness. A noble Bethel was built for him, a house of large dimensions, a fit sphere for his operations, and by his soul-stirring ministry he made "the Bethel" famous in all lands.

It was not at all wonderful that sailors especially, and other classes of the community in proportion, should flock to hear Mr. Taylor, for he was a man of great human sympathies, manly, bold, honest, childlike and outspoken; and, withal, a man on fire with love to Christ and perishing souls. His preaching never could be dull, the intense white heat of his nature prevented that. He was terribly in earnest, and commanded the attention of all around him for that very reason.

No ideas of propriety, or notions of delicacy, hung about him like fetters: he spoke to sailors, not to squeamish pomposity's, and to "the sons of Zebulon" he poured out his great heart in a homely eloquence, which was all on flame. One who heard him in 1835 said of him "His eloquence was marvelous: his control over the audience seemed almost absolute. Tears and smiles chased each other over our faces, like the rain and sunshine of an April day. He had one of the most brilliant imaginations that ever sparkled and burned. His sermon was all poetry, though it came in bursts and jets of flame. It was like the dance of the aurora, changing all the while from silver flame to purple, and back again. But the secret of his magnetic power lay in his overflowing sympathies, that leaped over all barriers, and had no regard for time or place. There was no wall of formality between him and his hearers, any more than if he were talking to each one of us in a private room. He would single out a person in his audience, and talk to him individually, with the same freedom as if he met him in the street. 'Ah! my jolly tar,' turning to a sailor who happened at that moment to catch his eye, 'here you are, in port again; God bless you! See to your helm, and you will reach a fairer port by-and-by. Hark! don't you hear the bells of heaven over the sea?'"

The ludicrous was allowed considerable play in his discourses, and we think rightly so. To the pure mind, none of the powers of our manhood are common or unclean. Humor can be consecrated, and should be. We grant that it is a power difficult to manage; but when it is under proper control, it more than repays for all the labor spent upon it. Children do sad damage with gunpowder; but what a force it is when a wise man directs its energy. Mr. Taylor made men laugh that they might weep. He touched one natural chord, that he might be able to touch another; whereas, some preachers are so unnatural themselves, that the human nature of their hearers refuses to subject itself to their operations. O ye who are evermore decorously dull, before ye judge a man whose loving ministry conducted thousands to the skies, think how immeasurably above you all he soared, and remember that with all his violations of your wretched regulations, he was one whom the Lord delighted to honor. Farthing candles rail at the sun for his spots, while they cannot be sure that those spots are not excessive light; and may be quite sure of another thing, that, spots or no spots, ten thousand such glimmers as theirs are not worthy to be compared with the stray beams of the great orb of day.

At the prayer-meetings Father Taylor, like a father in his family, cast off all restraint, and unveiled his inner nature with childlike unguardedness. One of his most remarkable displays of this kind was after an address by a visitor, who related the death of a very wicked man, who was blown up a few days before in a powder mill at Wilmington. He came down crushed and mangled, and gave his heart to God; and now who would not say with the holy man of old, "Let me die the death of the righteous, and let my last end be like his"? Father Taylor rose at once. "I don't want any trash brought unto this altar. I hope none of my people calculate on serving the devil all their lives and cheating him with their dying breath. Don't look forward to honoring God by giving him the last snuff of an expiring candle. *Perhaps you never will be blown up in a powder-mill."* "That holy man," he continued, "that we heard of was Balaam, the meanest scoundrel mentioned in the Old Testament or the New. And now I hope we shall never hear anything more from Balaam, *nor from his ass."*

His own prayers were more like the utterances of an Oriental, abounding in imagery, than a son of these colder western dimes. Think of his prayer at the dedication of a new church:—"If any man attempts to sow heresy in this pulpit, or to preach aught but Christ and him crucified, Lord drive him out of the house *and sweep his tracks off the floor."* The Sunday before he was to sail for Europe, he was en-treating the Lord to care well for his church during his absence. All at once he stopped and ejaculated, "What have I done? Distrust the Providence of heaven! A God that gives a whale a ton of herrings for a breakfast, will he not care for my children?" and then went on, closing his prayer in a more confiding strain.

"His work in one peculiar field is not, generally known. Living at the North End, near the lowest haunts of vice, he was often called to attend the death-beds of abandoned women. Protected by his eccentricity and his purity alike from any shadow of suspicion, he always obeyed such a summons. At all hours of the day or night he visited the foulest haunts of crime in this noble service; never with one harsh word for the fallen, never with any apology for their crime. He received many warnings against venturing on such errands. The only notice that he ever took of them was to lay aside his cane, which was elsewhere his constant companion, but which he never took with him when he visited the cellars and garrets of North Street. This was simple courage in the Christian soldier; but it was also the wisest prudence."

It grieves one's heart to relate that after many years of glorious service Father.Taylor faded away by degrees during ten long years, losing slowly all his powers. It was as the Lord would have it; but to drift about as a poor hulk, with the armament removed, and the light in the binnacle extinguished, was very grievous both to the old man and to his friends.

So passed away one whom Emerson called one of the two greatest poets of the United states. He was a Pedobaptist, an Arminian, and a man of a thousand divergences from our line of things, which we believe to be more Scriptural than his; but, for all that, upon the coffin of a good man and true, with no grudging hand we cast a funeral wreath, and say, "Would God there were others to fill his place!"

13
Edward Brooke, 1779—1871

OUR WESLEYAN BRETHREN HAVE lately lost from their ministry an eminently useful preacher, who was the last survivor of a little band of simple-hearted and downright earnest men, who in their day were mighty winners of souls, but had the reputation of being somewhat eccentric. 'William Dawson and Samuel Hick were worthily perpetuated in Squire Brooke, who entered into rest in January, 1871. We must not be supposed to endorse all his theology, or to hold up to admiration all his modes of procedure; but we have no patience with those who imagine that you cannot admire a man's character unless you agree with him in every doctrinal sentiment. Mr. Brooke was soundly abused in his day, and certain scurrilous papers imputed the most outrageous conduct to him; but, in truth, he was only a homely and somewhat quaint preacher of the old, old gospel, and his Master clothed him with great power.

Squire Brooke came of a substantial Yorkshire family, which possessed a considerable estate among the wild moorlands of the North. His parents belonged to the Established Church while Edward was in his boyhood, but were brought to know the Lord in after years by the preaching of their zealous son. Edward was not sent to Eton or Harrow, as he should have been; but following the bent of his inclination he was allowed to remain upon the farm, to fish, and hunt, and shoot, and to develop a fine constitution and an original mind. Amid the rocks and the heather, the forest trees and the ferns, Edward Brooke, with his dogs and his gun, found both sport and health; or dashing over the country after the hounds, he enjoy, eel exhilaration and trained his courage in the hunt. Up to the age of twenty-two he seems to have been devoid of religious thought; but as we Calvinists are wont to put it, the time appointed of the Lord drew near, and sovereign grace issued its writ of arrest against him, resolving in infinite love to make him a captive to its power.

"Early in the year 1821, Edward Brooke rose one morning, intent on pleasure. Equipped for his favorite sport, with gun in hand and followed by his dogs, he was crossing the Honley Moors, when a lone man met him with a message from God. The man was a Primitive Methodist preacher, named Thomas Holladay, one of those strong-minded, earnest evangelists, the validity of whose orders is disdainfully denied by many, but who, judged by the results of their ministry, hold a commission higher than bishops can bestow—a commission signed and sealed by him who is 'head over all things to his church.'

"Intent upon his Master's work, 'in season and out of season,' Holladay was prompt to seize an opportunity of usefulness. Passing the young sportsman, he respectfully saluted him, and said, with pitying earnestness,' Master, you are seeking happiness where you will never find it.' On went the man of God, perhaps little dreaming that the arrow thus shot at a venture had pierced the joints of the armor encasing the young sportsman's heart. Yet so it was.

"Home went the wounded sportsman, the words of Holladay still sounding in his ears, 'Master, you are seeking happiness where you will never find it.' The time was opportune. It was a day of visitation for that neighborhood. The Spirit of God was moving upon the population. A great revival was in progress.

The awakened young gentleman began to attend cottage prayer-meetings and to converse with the godly men of the neighborhood, and thus his anxiety was greatly deepened, and his desire for salvation inflamed.

"It was the day of his sister's wedding. Ill-prepared to join in the festivities of the occasion, because of the sorrow of his heart, Edward Brooke spent the previous night hours in reading his Bible and wrestling with God for salvation.

> All night the lonely suppliant prayed,
> All night his earnest crying made.

About four o'clock in the morning, whilst kneeling by the old armchair in his father's kitchen, still pleading for mercy through the mediation of Jesus, his soul grew desperate, and like Jacob wrestling with the angel till the break of day, he resolved, 'I will not let thee go except thou bless me.'

"That mighty importunity was the manifestation of true faith. He was enabled to receive Jesus as his Savior, and believing with the heart unto righteousness, these words were applied to his heart, as distinctly and impressively as though spoken by a voice from heaven: 'Thy sins which are many are all forgiven thee, go in peace and sin no more.' All fear and sorrow vanished, and, believing, he rejoiced with joy unspeakable and full of glory.

"Exulting in his wonderful deliverance, his first impulse was to make it known. He hastened to his sister's chamber and told her the glad news that Christ had saved him—a glorious announcement on her bridal morn: then, early though it was, he ran out into the village and roused a praying man called Ben Naylot, whose heart he knew would be in sympathy with his, and told him how he had found the Lord; and they two called up a third, named Joseph Donkersley, to share their joy; and from the rejoicing trio up went a song of praise, the jubilant and sweet notes of which were music in God's ear, and woke up the songs of angels, and gave new impulse to the happiness of heaven,' for there is joy in the presence of the angels of God over one sinner that repenteth,'"

From that moment Edward Brooke was what he would have called "a bran new man." He could do nothing by halves, and therefore he renounced once for all his former course of life, and finding field sports to have too great a charm for him, he gave them up in the most resolute manner. "Sir," said he to a Christian friend, "I found that the gate was strait, and so I pressed into it myself, and left my horses, and dogs, and the world outside." In his zeal to be quit of what he felt to be a temptation, he gave orders to have his dog kennels pulled down, on hearing which, his father interposed and countermanded the instructions, saying, "I hope Edward will want the kennels again"; but it was in vain, the die was cast, the camel had gone through the needle's eye, and could not come back through so narrow a passage. Edward Brooke frequented cottage prayer-meetings, talked with the workpeople at the mill, exhorted in his father's kitchen, and instructed wayfarers by the roadside; he began, in fact, to put himself in training to become "a mighty hunter before the Lord," a consecrated Nimrod whose game would be the souls of men.

Mr. Brooke's early career illustrates the great usefulness of small meetings in rooms and cottages, where the uneducated, the poor, and raw beginners may feel at home in their first attempts at speaking. Had it not been for such gatherings he might have remained silent, for he could not have dared to make his first essays before a large congregation. Our author wisely remarks that "The cottage prayer-meeting is certainly one of the best training schools for the development of Christian gifts. In some of our town-circuits, where chapels are few and large, and the pulpits invariably supplied by ordained ministers, and where Sunday afternoon services have been discontinued, and no rooms or cottages are opened for mission work, what opportunity have those whom the Spirit moves to preach his word, to test their call by actual experiment, and to develop their preaching power by frequent practice?

"In such meetings, Edward Brooke first ventured to deliver the message of salvation, which was as a burning fire shut up in his bones, till he was weary with forbearing and could not stay; and there he found encouragement and strength for further service.

"After prayerful consideration and consultation with Christian friends, it was arranged that Edward Brooke should submit his convictions of duty to the judgment of others, by preaching in James Donkersley's chamber, a large room which answered the threefold purpose of a workshop, a bedroom, and a place where the neighbors might gather to worship God. The service was duly announced, and great interest awakened in the young squire's first appearance as a preacher. The chamber was thronged, and many a heart uplifted in earnest prayer that God would encourage and help his young servant in this first trial of his pulpit gifts. The preacher took for his text a passage in harmony with his intense convictions: 'The wicked shall be turned into hell.' Acting upon a sense of duty, and humbly relying on God, the preacher was divinely assisted, and the effort was a success.

"The news that the young squire had begun to preach soon spread through the neighborhood and district, and created no small sensation. Opportunity to exercise his gifts offered on every hand, which he accepted as a call from God. Those who had known the squire in his wild days, and those who had heard of his remarkable conversion, all flocked to hear him. The announcement that Squire Brooke would preach, not only drew young squires, but emptied the public houses far and near, and was the signal for many an old poacher, dog-fighter, pigeon-flyer, drunkard, and habitual Sabbath-breaker, to find his way to the house of God. The squire attracted congregations such as no other man could get, comprising the fast men, the publicans and harlots, the roughs and outcasts of society, the sight of whom, in the house of God, must have made the heart of the preacher leap for joy, and carried him out of himself.

"Influenced by the strange character of the congregations which thronged to hear him, and by the fact that many heard him, to whose untaught, sensual minds, theological terms and doctrinal definitions conveyed no meaning, and ordinary preaching was unintelligible, he, of set purpose, renounced the style of his first sermon in favor of another, which but for the preacher's motive and exceptional position, might be open to criticism, and which, in a copyist, would be most reprehensible."

We cannot pretend to give even an outline of Mr. Brooke's long and useful life, but must content ourselves with citing incidents which illustrate both his eccentricity and fervor. He gradually relinquished all his secular pursuits for the sake of soul-winning, and having an ample fortune he traveled far and wide, bearing his own charges, and preaching the gospel without money and without price, a mode of life which we both admire and envy. In his rambles, and at other times, he was always on the look-out for individual cases, with which he dealt in his own fashion, and with remarkable success. Note the following:—

One of the members of the Sheepridge Society unhappily tampered with strong drink, till his enemy got the advantage of him. He was found one day, in a public-house, indulging in free potations; and his wife's persuasions failing to bring him out, she came to the squire to ask his interference.

"Away went the squire forthwith, conducted by the sorrowing woman, and, reaching the house, he walked straight into the bar, where a number of old topers were soaking according to their custom; and there, in their midst, was the fallen man. 'What art thou doing here?' said the squire, fixing his eyes upon the poor backslider, 'this is no place for thee.' Disconcerted by Mr. Brooke's unexpected appearance, and consciencestricken, the man gave no reply, and seemed as though he would fain have dropped through the floor to escape the terrible gaze of the squire's reproving eyes. 'Come out with me and come home with me,' said the squire, and as the culprit still kept his seat, he seized him by his coat collar and pulled him out into the street."

"The topers, exasperated by such infringement of the 'liberty of the subject,' sprang to their feet and rushed to the rescue. The squire turned himself about, looked his opponents in the face, and raising his big, powerful arm, said, 'There is not a man in the lot dare lay a finger on me.' He then walked off his captive, gave him good counsel, and there is reason to believe that he never fell into the snare again."

"Driving to an appointment on a flue Sabbath morning in spring, with Mr. D. Smith, a Sheffield local preacher and a colleague in labor, Mr. Brooke suddenly said, 'Pall up, Smith.' Mr. Brooke then stood up in the conveyance and shouted to a man in a distant part of a field by the wayside, who was gathering nettles, 'Here, I want thee,' beckoning with his hand at the same time for the man to come to him, When he came up to the fence, Mr. Brooke said,' Thou poor foolish sinner, art thou going to sell thy precious soul to the devil on a Sunday morning for a few paltry nettles!' and looking earnestly into his face, he prayed with great solemnity, 'The Lord have mercy on thy soul. Amen.' Then, quick as thought, he said,' Drive on, Smith.' When fairly on the way again, he said, 'I could not let that man sell his soul for nettles without warning him.'" "Driving to some village in

Derbyshire, where he was expected to preach in the after part of the day, the squire pulled up at a wayside inn. Having seen his horse fed, he ordered his usual refreshment of ham and eggs. A fine, healthy-looking young countryman entered the room and sat down to rest. The squire made some friendly observations, and when his repast was spread, invited the young man to join him. The offer was gratefully accepted. Whilst enjoying their savory dish the youth's heart opened, and there was a pleasant flow of conversation. 'We are expecting a very strange preacher,' said he,' at our village to-night. He is a great man for prayer-meetings, and tries to convert all the folks into Methodists.' 'Indeed,' replied the squire, with evident interest in the topic, 'have you ever heard him?' 'No, I haven't,' said the youth, 'but my brother has.' 'Well, what did your brother say about him?' enquired the squire. 'Oh, he told me he never heard such a queer chap in his life; indeed, he didn't know if he were quite right in his head; but,' said the young man, 'I intend to go and hear for myself.' 'That is right, my lad,' said the squire, 'and get your brother to go too, he may have a word to suit you both.' They did go, and greatly to the young man's surprise, as the preacher mounted the pulpit, he recognized his friendly entertainer at the wayside inn. As the squire proceeded with the service the young man's heart was touched, and his brothers also. At the prayer-meeting they were found amongst the penitent seekers of salvation, and were both converted not merely into Methodists, but into Christian believers."

Here is a specimen of his characteristic letters: brief, but all on fire:—

"Dear John,—In reply to yours, I beg leave to say that our labor at Honley was not in vain. A new class has been formed, and about a dozen have gone to it. Two found peace. Praise the Lord! We shall rise. All hell is on the move, but we must go round about the bulwarks of our Zion, and mark well her palaces, and we shall ultimately and finally triumph over all. I say all. Go on, John, in the work. Live near to God. Be a giant in religion; one of the first and best men in your day. Plead with God. Live in the glory. 'Advance' is the Christian's motto. Onward to certain victory over sin, the world, and hell. Trample down worldly, fashionable conformity. Know the will of Got and do it. Do it heartily, cheerfully, fully, eternally, and heaven will be your guide, defense, and all in all. Our kind respects.

"And in your prayers, remember

"EDWARD BROOKE."

We take farewell of Squire Brooke with regret, as we copy the last entry from his diary:—"'In returning and rest shall ye be saved: in quietness and in confidence shall be your strength.'—'Thou shalt see greater things than these.'—'Thou preventest him with the blessings of goodness.'—'I will do better unto you than at your beginnings.'—'My soul is even as a weaned child.' And then, possibly to express his fuller apprehension of the infinite mercy of his covenant God, and a firmer trust than he had heretofore exercised, he writes with a trembling hand that was soon to forget its cunning, 'Never before.'"

We do not wonder that his memoir is in the fourth thousand ("Squire Brooke," by the Rev. J. H. Lord. Hamilton, Adams and Co.); it is exceedingly well written, and we congratulate Mr. Lord upon his spirit and ability.

14
Billy Bray, The Uneducated Soul-winner

MANY CHRISTIANS WHO ARE prepared to tolerate, and even to admire considerable diversities of character, have yet, unconsciously to themselves, laid down in their own minds very fixed and definite limits within which those diversities shall range. So far they are still looking for a measure of uniformity, and will probably require several more or less violent wrenches of their propriety before they will be able to admit within the circle of their sympathy sundry eccentric and erratic forms of genuine spiritual life, which, nevertheless, have had their uses, and have brought no small glory to God. We are most of us somewhat tolerant of well-educated eccentrics; we almost reverence the oddities of genius, but we are squeamish if we see singularities combined with ignorance, and idiosyncrasies prominent in men who cannot even spell the word. What in a gentleman would be a peculiarity, is reckoned in a poor man to be an absurdity. Such slaves are most men to kid gloves and good balances at the banker's, that they toady to aristocratic whims, and even affect to admire in my Lord Havethecash that which would disgust them in poor Tom Honesty. This partiality of judgment, in a measure, affects even Christians, who, beyond all other men, are bound to judge things by their own intrinsic value, and not according to the false glitter of position and wealth. We claim for uneducated Christian men as wide a range for their originality as would be allowed them if they were the well-instructed sons of the rich; we would not have a shrewd saying decried because it is ungrammatical; nor a fervent, spiritual utterance ridiculed because it is roughly expressed. Consider the man as he is; make allowances for educational disadvantages, for circumstances, and for companionships, and do not turn away with contempt from that which, in the sight of God, may be infinitely more precious than all the refinements and delicacies so dear to pompous imbecility.

With this long-winded preface we now introduce a few notes upon William Bray, of Cornwall, for several years a local preacher among the Bible Christians: we beg his pardon for calling him by a name which he never used, and introduce him a second time, with due accuracy, as *Billy Bray*. This worthy was once a drunken and lascivious miner, but grace made him an intensely earnest and decided follower of the Lord Jesus. His conversion was very marked, and was attended with those violent struggles of conscience which frequently attend that great change in strong-minded and passionate natures.

His actual obtaining of peace brought the tears into our eyes as we read it, and made us remember a lad who, more than twenty years ago, found the Lord in a somewhat similar style; it also reminded us of George Fox the Quaker, and John Bunyan the Baptist, when undergoing the sacred change. Children of God are born very much alike; their divergences usually arise as a matter of after years. In their regeneration, as in their prayers, they appear as one. Bray was assailed by the fierce temptation that he would never find mercy; but with the promise, "Seek, and ye shall find," he quenched this fiery dart of the wicked one, and in due time he learned, by blessed experience, that the promise was true. Beautifully simple and touching are his own words:—"I said to the Lord, 'Thou hast said, *They that ask shall receive, they that seek shall find, and to them that knock the door shall be opened,* and I have faith to believe it.' In an instant the Lord made me so happy that I cannot express what I felt. I shouted for joy. I praised God with my whole heart for what he had done for a poor sinner like me: for I could say, the Lord hath pardoned all my sins. I think this was in November, 1823, but what day of the month I do not know. I remember this, that everything looked new to me; the people, the fields, the cattle, the trees. I was like a man in a new world. I spent the greater part of my time in praising the Lord. I could say with David, 'The Lord hath brought me up out of a horrible pit, and out of the miry clay, and set my feet upon a rock, and established my goings, and hath put a new song in my mouth, even praise unto my God.' I was a new man altogether. I told all I met what the Lord had done for my soul. I have heard some say that they have hard work to get away from their companions, but I had hard work to find them soon enough to tell them what the Lord had done for me. Some said I was mad; and others that they should get me back again next pay-day. But, praise the Lord, it is now more than forty years ago, and they have not got me yet. They said I was a *mad*-man, but they meant I was a *glad* man, and, glory be to God! I hare been glad ever since."

No sooner was Billy saved than he began at once looking after others. He prayed for his work-mates, and saw several brought to Jesus in answer to his prayer. His was a simple faith; he believed in the reality of prayer, and meant to be heard, and expected to be answered whenever he supplicated for the souls of his comrades. He was a live man, not a dummy. In his own simple style he did all that he did with rigor, physical vigor being more than sufficiently conspicuous in his shouting and leaping for joy. "He tells us, soon after his conversion, 'I was very happy in my work, and could leap and dance for joy underground as well as on the surface.'

"Bray began publicly to exhort men to repent, and turn to God, about a year after his conversion. Towards the end of 1824 his name was put on the Local Preachers' Plan, and his labors were much blessed in the conversion of souls. He did not commonly select a text, as is the general habit of preachers, but he usually began his addresses by reciting a verse of a hymn, a little of his own experience, or some telling anecdote. But he had the happy art of pleasing and profiting all classes, the rich as much as the poor; and all characters, the worldly as much as the pious, flocked to' hear him. He retained his popularity until the last. Perhaps no preacher in Cornwall ever acquired more extensive or more lasting renown, and the announcement of his name as a speaker at a missionary meeting, or on any special occasion, was a sufficient attraction, whoever else might or might not be present. Sometimes his illustrations and appeals made a powerful impression. I remember once hearing him speak with great effect to a large congregation, principally miners. In that neighborhood there were two mines, one very prosperous, and the other quite the reverse, for the work was hard and the wages low. In his sermon he represented himself as working at *that* mine all the week, but on the' pay-day' going to the prosperous one for his wages. Had he not been at work at the other mine? the manager inquired. He had, but he liked the wages at the good mine the best. He pleaded very earnestly, but in vain, and was dismissed with the remark, from which there was no appeal, that he must come there to work if he came there for his wages. And then he turned upon the congregation, and the effect was almost irresistible, that they must serve Christ here if they would share his glory hereafter, but if they would serve the devil now, to him they must go for their wages byand- by. A very homely illustration certainly, but one which convinced the understanding and subdued the hearts of his hearers.

"There was excitement in some of his meetings, more than sufficient to shock the prejudices of highly-sensitive or refined persons. Some even who had the fullest confidence and warmest affection for Billy could not enjoy some of the outward manifestations they occasionally witnessed to the extent that he himself did. Billy could not tolerate 'deadness,' as he expressively called it, either in a professing Christian or in a meeting. He had a,leeper sympathy with persons singing, or shouting, or leaping for joy, than he had with

'The speechless awe that dares not move,
And all the silent heaven of love.'"

Methodism is the mother church of Cornwall, and Bray was a genuine though uncultivated child of her heart. As John Wesley always associated the grace of God with the penny a week, so Bray's religion was not all shouting; it had an eminently practical turn in many directions. Billy was quite a mighty chapel builder; he began by getting a piece of freehold from his mother, which he cleared with his own hands, and then proceeded to dig out the foundations of a chapel which was to be called *Bethel*. Under great discouragement's, both from friends and foes, mostly, however, from the first, he actually built the place, working at it himself, and at the same time begging stone, begging timber, and begging money to pay the workmen. His little all he gave, and moved all around, who had anything to spare, to give likewise. On-lookers thought Billy to be silly, and called him so; but, as he well remarked, "Wise men could not have preached in the chapel if silly Billy had not built it." Almost as soon as one building was finished, he was moved to commence another. It was much needed, and many talked about it, but nobody had the heart to begin it but Billy Bray. He begged the land, borrowed a horse and cart of the giver; and then after doing his own hard day's work underground in the pit, and providing for five small children, he and his son worked at raising stone and building the walls; frequently working twenty hours of the twenty-four. He had a hard struggle over this second chapel; but his own account is best. "When our chapel was up about to the door-head, the devil said to me, 'They are all gone and left you and the chapel, and I would go and leave the place too.' Then I said, 'Devil, doesn't thee know me better than that; by the help of the Lord I will have the chapel up, or lose my skin on the down.' So the devil said no more to me on that subject. Sometimes I had blisters on my hands, and they have been very sore. But I felt I did not mind that, for if the chapel should stand one hundred years, and if one soul were converted in it every year, *that* would be a hundred souls, and that would pay me well if I got to heaven, for they that 'turn many to righteousness shall shine as the stars for ever and ever.' So I thought I should be rich enough when I got there. The chapel was finished after a time; and the opening day came. We had preaching, but the preacher was a wise man, and a dead man. I believe there was not much good done that day, for it was a very dead time with the preacher and people; for he had a great deal of *grammar*, and but little of *Father*. 'It is not by might, nor power, but by my Spirit, saith the

Lord' Weir it was by wisdom or might, I should have but a small part, for my might is little and my wisdom less. Thanks be to God, the work is his, and he can work by whomsoever he pleases. The second Sunday after the chapel was opened I was 'planned' there. I said to the people, 'You know I did not work here about this chapel in order to fill my pocket, but for the good of the neighbors, and the good of souls; and souls I must have, and souls I will have.' The Lord blessed us in a wonderful manner. Two women cried to the Lord for mercy; and when I saw *that* I said, 'Now the chapel is paid for already.' The good Lord went on to work there; and the society soon went up from fifteen members to thirty. You see how good the Lord is to me; I spoke for one soul a year, and he gave me fifteen souls the first year. Bless and praise his holy name, for he is good, and his mercy endureth for ever, for one soul is worth a thousand worlds. Our little chapel had three windows, one on one side, and two on the other; the old devil, who does not like chapels, put his servants, by way of reproach, to call our chapel *Three-Eyes*. But, blessed be God, since then the chapel has become too small for the place; and it has been enlarged; now there are six windows instead of three; and they may call the chapel *Six-Eyes* if they will. For, glory be to God, many that have been converted there are now in heaven; and, when we get there, we will praise him with all our might; and *he shall never hear the last of it.*"

No sooner was this second house finished, than he began a third and larger one, and in this enterprise his talent for collecting, as well as his zeal in giving and working, were well displayed. He had high—and as we believe proper—ideas of his mission, in gathering in the subscriptions of the Lord's stewards. "A friend who was with Billy on a begging expedition, suggested, as they were coming near a gentleman's house, and Billy was evidently making for the front door, that it would be better if they went to the back door. 'No,' said Billy, 'I am the son of a King, and I shall go frontways.'" "At one time, at a missionary meeting, he seemed quite vexed because there was something said in the report about money received for 'rags and bones.' when he rose to address the meeting he said: 'I don't think it is right supporting the Lord's cause with old rags and bones. The Lord deserves the best, and ought to have the best.'" Well done, Billy! This is right good, and sound divinity.

Billy knew how to fight the devil and his agents with their own weapons. Returning late from a revival meeting, on a dark night in a lonely road, "certain lewd fellows of the baser sort," tried to frighten him by making all sorts of unearthly sounds; but he went singing on his way. At last one of them said, in the most terrible tones, "But I'm the devil up here in the hedge, Billy Bray." "Bless the Lord! Bless the Lord!" said Billy, *"I did not know thee 'wust' so far away as that."* To use Billy's own expression, "What could the devil do with such as he?"

"One of the most blessed results of his deep piety was his unfeigned humility, and his continual sense of dependence upon God. The Lord's servants without the Lord's presence are weak like other men, like Samson, when he lost his locks. Here is one experience of Billy's: 'When I was in the St. Neot's Circuit, I was on the plan; and I remember that one Sunday I was planned at Redgate, and there was a chapel full of people, and the Lord gave me great power and liberty in speaking; but all at once the Lord took away his Spirit from me, so that I could not speak a word: and this might have been the best sermon that some of them ever heard. What! you say, and you looking like a fool and not able to speak? Yes, for it was not long before I said, I am glad I am stopped, and that for *three* reasons. And the first is, To humble my soul, and make me feel more dependent on my Lord, to think more fully of the Lord and less of myself. The next reason is, To convince you that are ungodly, for you say we can speak what we have a mind to, without the Lord as well as with him; but you cannot say so now, for you hear how I was speaking, but when the Lord took away his Spirit I could not say another word; without my Lord I could do nothing. And the third reason is, That some of you young men who are standing here may be called to stand in the pulpit some day as I am, and the Lord may take his Spirit from you as he has from me, and then you might say, it is no good for me to try to preach or exhort, for I was stopped the last time I tried to preach, and I shall preach no more. But now you can say, I saw poor old Billy Bray stopped once like me, and he did not mind it, and told the people that he was glad his Lord had stopped him: Billy Bray's Lord is my Lord, and I am glad he stopped me too, for if I can benefit the people and glorify God, that is what I want. I then spoke a great while, and told the people what the Lord gave me to say.'"

Preaching in such a spirit Bray was sure to have a blessing, and a blessing he had. Many orators and doctors in divinity look very small by the side of Billy Bray, if we estimate ministries by their results in soul-winning, and they will look smaller still when the souls saved by poor humble speakers shall shine forth like stars, and their own rhetorical fame and boasted learning shall be as darkness.

We say no more, but refer the reader to the memoir of Billy Bray, written by Mr. F.W. Bourne, and published at the Bible Christian Book Room, 57, Fairbank Street, East Road.

15
In Conclusion

ALL THESE ECCENTRIC PREACHERS were in downright earnest, and because they were so their humor sometimes came to the front. Had their consecration to their work been less complete they would have taken more thought of public opinion, and have been more fearful of incurring reproach; but they were so set upon their one object of sending home the truth to the consciences of their hearers that they forgot their own reputations, and spoke with boldness.

Had these men been triflers with holy things, or jesters upon sacred topics, they would have been worthy of all the censure which has been poured upon them; but they were nothing of the kind. Among the earnest they were the most earnest; no one can doubt that. This, indeed, lay at the bottom of the opposition which they aroused. Had they been mere jesters the world would not have hated them so much as it did, for it loves those who make it sport. Had they cultivated a prim feebleness, or had they been content to discharge their office with the lifelessness of routine, they would have run no risk of standing in the pillory of scorn, for men may be as dull and as powerless as they please in the ministry without fear of being called eccentric.

If all men were right-minded they would be willing to listen to the message of salvation, even if it were couched in the driest terms of technical theology; but men are so careless about all the matters of their souls that we have not only to preach to them, but to induce them to hear us. A great part of our labor lies in seeking out attractive illustrations, parables, and choice sayings, by which we may coax men to attend to their own interests; and even then we fail unless a higher power intervenes. We would be content to preach didactic truth with unvarying solemnity if the multitude would but hear us, but they will not. What then? If the healing medicine is nauseous to the child, we must sweeten the draught or gild the pill. If our words will not run by themselves, we must put them on wheels and so set them in motion. Our object is—if by any means we may save some; and since men will not believe without hearing, and will not hear unless we make the word pleasant and attractive to them, we dare not do otherwise than indulge them in this respect, and woo them to instruction as children are enticed to learning by stories and pictures.

This little book is not written to inculcate eccentricity, or even to excuse all its displays; but, if possible, to take the edge from the scalping knife of slanderous misrepresentation and carping censure. Fair and honest criticism is not to be deprecated; it may be useful if honestly and kindly spoken. No Christian minister in his right mind wishes to shield himself behind his office, nor does he desire to be regarded as infallible; but what we do request is that our hearers' thoughts should not be diverted from our subject by the little details of our style and manner. These are trifles, but our message is a matter of life and death.

Reader, if you are brought to believe in the Lord Jesus Christ you will find rely little fault with the ministry which has led to so desirable a consummation; and if you are a hearer of the gospel and still reject the Savior, you will not be able to make an excuse for your unbelief out of the singularity of the preacher, for in these days if one man cannot profit you it is easy for you to find another, and there is no law to prevent your going where you are most benefited. Better shift your seat than waste your Sabbaths.

To all wise and candid believers we commend the language of the apostle,—as the Lord gave to every man?" They are not to be pitted one against another, as if they were rivals engaged in fighting for the belt, they are to be loved, helped, and prayed for as fellow-helpers of our faith. "Therefore let no man glory in men, (or despise them either,) for all things are yours, whether Paul, or Apollos, or Cephas, or the world, or life, or death, or things present, or things to come; all are yours; and ye are Christ's; and Christ is God's."

Eccentric Preachers

Printed in Great Britain
by Amazon